THRIVE

3/1/2014

Congratulations and best of luck!

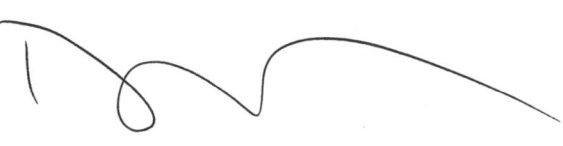

ADVANCE PRAISE FOR

THRIVE
A NEW LAWYER'S GUIDE TO LAW FIRM PRACTICE

"A VERY USEFUL GUIDE, WITH HIGHLY PRACTICAL TIPS FOR ANYONE CONSIDERING OR STARTING A LAW FIRM CAREER."

JULIE MATLOF KENNEDY, OF COUNSEL FOR LITIGATION TRAINING, MORRISON FOERSTER LLP

"DO YOU FEEL LIKE YOU KNOW THE UNSPOKEN RULES OF LAW FIRM PRACTICE? IF NOT, YOU NEED TO READ THIS BOOK. CHOCK FULL OF ESSENTIAL ADVICE ON WHAT TO DO (AND WHAT NOT TO DO) IN YOUR FIRST YEARS AT THE FIRM, IT WILL SAVE YOU FROM ALL THE IMPENDING DISASTERS YOU DIDN'T EVEN KNOW WERE COMING AT YOU. FOREWARNED IS FOREARMED!"

ALISON MONAHAN, FOUNDER, GIRL'S GUIDE TO LAW SCHOOL & LAW SCHOOL TOOLBOX

"*THRIVE* IS AN INVALUABLE RESOURCE FOR NAVIGATING THE CHALLENGES ENCOUNTERED DAILY BY THE NEW PRACTITIONER AND CONTAINS A HOST OF STREET SMARTS TYPICALLY ACQUIRED ONLY THROUGH TRIAL AND ERROR. THE ONLY THING MISSING IS A SPORTS PAGE. STAY TUNED."

RICHARD A. SIEBEL, RETIRED JUDGE, CIRCUIT COURT OF COOK COUNTY, ILLINOIS

"*THRIVE* IS JAM PACKED WITH SPOT-ON ADVICE FOR NEW LAWYERS, PARTICULARLY FOR THOSE JOINING PRIVATE LAW FIRMS. BOTH PRACTICAL AND DO-ABLE, THE ADVICE SHARED HERE SHOULD BE ADOPTED BY ALL FIRST YEAR ASSOCIATES AND CARRIED OUT FROM DAY ONE. *THRIVE* IS A 'MUST-READ'!"

SANDRA BANG, DIRECTOR OF GLOBAL LEGAL TALENT DEVELOPMENT AT SHEARMAN & STERLING LLP

"DESIRÉE MOORE ARTFULLY DELIVERS A ROAD MAP FOR LEGAL SUCCESS IN THE NEW MILLENNIUM. SHE OFFERS READERS AN INSIDE LOOK AT THE COMPLEXITY OF PROSPERING IN A TRANSFORMED LEGAL INDUSTRY WHILE SHARING CONCRETE ADVICE FOR NAVIGATING A VARIETY OF PROFESSIONAL ROLES, COLLABORATING WITH COLLEAGUES, AND LEVERAGING TECHNOLOGY TO RAISE YOUR PROFILE."

ARI KAPLAN, AUTHOR, REINVENTING PROFESSIONAL SERVICES: BUILDING YOUR BUSINESS IN THE DIGITAL MARKETPLACE (WILEY, 2011)

"DESIRÉE MOORE HAS WRITTEN A MANUSCRIPT THAT WILL HELP INEXPERIENCED LAWYERS NOT ONLY SURVIVE BUT EXCEL IN THEIR FIRST DELICATE AND FORMATIVE YEARS. THE MATERIAL IS WELL PLANNED, AND NECESSARY FOR THE NOVICE TO ACHIEVE THE GOAL OF BECOMING A SUCCESSFUL PRACTITIONER IN THE ART OF LAWYERING. AN UNDENIABLY EXCELLENT BOOK . . . WELL DONE!"

DANIEL E. BRYAN JR. DISTRICT JUDGE, FIRST JUDICIAL DISTRICT, STATE OF NEBRASKA

"FEW STATIONS IN A PROFESSIONAL'S LIFE ARE AS ANXIETY-RIDDEN AS BEING A NEW LAWYER. DESIRÉE MOORE DISAGGREGATES AND THEN TAMES SOURCES OF THE ANXIETY. THEY WILL NEVER BE THE SAME. *THRIVE* IS A MUST-READ FOR NEW LAWYERS."

PETE KALIS, GLOBAL MANAGING PARTNER, K&L GATES

Cover by Kelly Book/ABA Publishing.

The materials contained herein represent the opinions and views of the authors and/or the editors, and should not be construed to be the views or opinions of the law firms or companies with whom such persons are in partnership with, associated with, or employed by, nor of the Young Lawyers Division, unless adopted pursuant to the bylaws of the Association.

Nothing contained in this book is to be considered as the rendering of legal advice for specific cases, and readers are responsible for obtaining such advice from their own legal counsel. This book is intended for educational and informational purposes only.

© 2012 American Bar Association. All rights reserved.

No part of this publication may be reproduced, stored in a retrieval system, or transmitted in any form or by any means, electronic, mechanical, photocopying, recording, or otherwise, without the prior written permission of the publisher. For permission, contact the ABA Copyrights and Contracts Department by e-mail at copyright@americanbar.org or fax at 312-988-6030, or complete the online request form at http://www.abanet.org/utility/reprints.html.

Printed in the United States of America

16 15 14 13   5 4 3 2

Library of Congress Cataloging-in-Publication Data

Moore, Desiree.

  Thrive : a new lawyers guide to law firm practice / Desiree Moore.

     p. cm.

  ISBN 978-1-61438-743-5

 1. Law--Vocational guidance--United States. 2. Law offices--United

States. 3. Practice of law--United States. I. Title.

  KF297.M66 2012

  340.023'73--dc23

                                                      2012037910

Discounts are available for books ordered in bulk. Special consideration is given to state bars, CLE programs, and other bar-related organizations. Inquire at Book Publishing, ABA Publishing, American Bar Association, 321 North Clark Street, Chicago, Illinois 60654-7598.

www.ShopABA.org

FOR ABRAM AND THE
PEANUT, MY DARLINGS.

CONTENTS

ACKNOWLEDGEMENTS	XV
CHAPTER 1 ON THE BENEFITS OF COACHING	1
CHAPTER 2 THE NEW LAWYER EXPERIENCE AND A NOTE ABOUT TRIBES	3
CHAPTER 3 YOUR MIND-SET	7

CHAPTER 4
YOUR ROLE IN A LAW FIRM — 13

CHAPTER 5
PROFESSIONALISM — 19

CHAPTER 6
LITIGATION VERSUS TRANSACTIONAL PRACTICE — 27

CHAPTER 7
LAW FIRM STRUCTURE — 31

CHAPTER 8
MENTORSHIP — 39

CHAPTER 9
TIME MANAGEMENT AND ORGANIZATION — 43

CHAPTER 10
WORKING WITH STAFF — 51

CHAPTER 11
WORKING WITH ATTORNEYS — 61

CHAPTER 12
SPEAKING LIKE A LAWYER — 73

CHAPTER 13
WRITING LIKE A LAWYER — 79

CHAPTER 14
FEEDBACK — 93

CHAPTER 15
MISTAKES — 99

CHAPTER 16
MARKETING — 103

CHAPTER 17
SOCIAL MEDIA AND YOUR LEGAL PRACTICE — 111

CHAPTER 18
HEALTH AND WELLNESS — 117

CHAPTER 19
ON LEADERSHIP — 121

APPENDIX 1
SAMPLE E-MAIL — 123

APPENDIX 2
SAMPLE LETTER — 127

APPENDIX 3
SAMPLE TIME ENTRIES — 131

INDEX — 137

ABOUT THE AUTHOR — 149

ACKNOWLEDGEMENTS

I loved writing this book. And I am honored to share it with you. As I make my final edits and turn this book over to be published, my deepest expression of thanks and gratitude goes to: my parents, Norman and Maura Furman, for giving and loving and supporting unconditionally; my sisters, Arianne and Fabianne Furman, for a shared work ethic, shared perspective, and genuine enthusiasm for all of my projects; and my husband, Abram Moore, for being more impressive than I could have ever imagined. For his openness, too, and for his love, his support of my various endeavors, for giving me time and space to try this, and for just about everything else.

I'd also like to thank: Seth Godin for writing *Tribes: We Need You to Lead Us*; John Rotunno, whose practice habits are impeccable and who taught me by example how to practice law; Daniel Hayes, for mentorship, friendship, and a foray into the ministry so Abe and I could walk down the aisle; Sara Fletcher, my unofficial editor and dear friend; and everyone else who read chapters of this book and weighed in with comments, suggestions, revisions, and proposed titles of their own. A special thanks to Pete Kalis, Ari Kaplan, Judge Richard Siebel, Judge Daniel Bryan, Sandra Bang, Alison Monahan, and Julie Matlof Kennedy, whose good words grace the cover of this book. A big thank you also to my editor, Erin Nevius, who has been a pleasure to work with, and to the American Bar Association for publishing me!

Finally, thank you to Loyola University Chicago School of Law. All of the good things that have come in recent years can be traced back, in one way or another, to my time at Loyola.

It's been fun. Lots more where this came from. Come with me?

With love and gratitude,
Desirée

1

ON THE BENEFITS OF COACHING

Last fall, there was a great article in *The New Yorker* about the value of coaching. The author, a surgeon who had been practicing for eight years, enlisted a former professor to coach him through a series of surgeries and help him improve his technique and skill. Athletes and singers have coaches, the author reasoned, so why not the rest of us? The professor's coaching advice was subtle—he was coaching a seasoned professional after all—but there was plenty to be said and learned anyway.[1]

I loved this piece. And, in some ways, it is the very premise of

---

1 Atul Gawande, *Annals of Medicine: Personal Best*, NEW YORKER, Oct. 3, 2011, at 44-53.

this book. As a law school graduate, you are highly trained—and trained to think differently than nonlawyers. You are adept at spotting legal implications and legal consequences. You are well read, have a profound endurance for reading tedious materials, and have impeccable knowledge of black letter law. You are, by definition, a professional and a member of one of the most distinguished professions of all time.

Still, there is so much room for guidance and improvement. You, like the surgeon, can benefit from a coach, from someone who is watching over you as you embark on your legal career. What's more, with the supply of lawyers being wildly disproportionate to demand and with law schools not preparing lawyers to actually practice law (this is not even the purpose of a law school education, as I'm sure you have gathered by now), you can use whatever edge you can get. If you are open to it, then, the contents of this book will enlighten you, improve your performance, save you some very real growing pains, and accelerate your legal career.

2

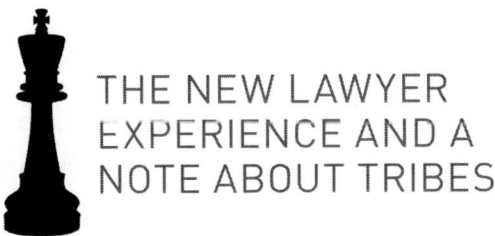

THE NEW LAWYER EXPERIENCE AND A NOTE ABOUT TRIBES

I graduated from law school in 2005. Out of law school, I went to work for a midsize law firm. Later, my firm merged with a megafirm with thousands of attorneys worldwide.

I was with my firm for nearly seven years. In seven years, I knew nothing; learned a lot; struggled some (the word *struggled* has a bit of a negative connotation—the thesaurus suggests that I use *gave it the old college try* instead, which I thought was funny, but I guess you could say that); made amazing friends; worked hard; saw a huge market downturn; second-chaired a four-week-long jury trial (thank you, Dave); recruited, trained, and mentored many incoming lawyers; and billed upward of thirteen thousand hours.

Now that, my friends—that intensive law firm experience, those hours and hours of practice—makes me an expert. Not an expert practitioner. (Do those exist? In any event, I'm definitely not one.) But an expert in the new lawyer experience. An expert in how to master the early years of legal practice in a law firm. An expert in how to be engaging, impressive, driven, and successful in your early career. How to stand apart from your colleagues. How to build a reputation as a superstar associate. How to thrive. I am close enough to the new lawyer experience to describe exactly what you need to know to be a successful associate today. And this is why we are here: I want to teach you what I've learned.

Seth Godin writes about tribes,[1] groups of people who share something in common—passion, interest, circumstance, ideas—just waiting for an opportunity to be brought together. There are tribes everywhere in search of communities, of leaders, he says, and here we are.

In thinking about this principle as I write, it occurs to me that lawyers are a tribe of sorts. But it is a peculiar tribe. Three years of law school and the bar exam are rites of passage—and these experiences funnel you into a tribe almost involuntarily. In retrospect, the whole process is a bit like one of those slides at a water park where you head down a dark tunnel feet first, flat on your back with your arms crossed against your chest, and your speed picks up and you ride erratically up the sides of the slide and your legs splay and you wonder if you're going a bit too fast or if you would choose to go again if given the option and then, there's a crack of light, and you're shot out into a pool just deep enough to dunk you

---

[1] Seth Godin, Tribes: We Need You to Lead Us (2008).

for a second.

As lawyers, this is our tribe. Or at least how our tribe is formed. How it *feels*. We're all in this pool just over our heads enough that we're distressed, but not enough that we turn to the tribe for help. Instead, we just swim. And we're not a tribe in the sense that we've rallied together. No. We just found ourselves here.

But now, here, and with you, I'd like to try this differently. This book was written for a different tribe. A subset of the tribe "lawyers." This is for lawyers who are just beginning their careers, who want to do more than show up, act eagerly, and not get fired. This is for lawyers who want to take their careers head on, with direction and purpose. This is for lawyers who want to know what their role is in a law firm from day one, not to happen upon it as time goes by. This is for you if you don't care to be frustrated or overwhelmed by your career, but awakened. This is for you if you want to be a leader in your law firm or practice area or industry, five, ten, or twenty years down the line. This is for you if you give a damn. This is for *that* tribe. Are you in?

3

YOUR MIND-SET

Your daily interactions in a law firm are full of opportunities—opportunities to be impressive, engaging, and indispensable. Your job is to identify those opportunities. In order to do this, you have to be in the right frame of mind. And this entails three specific things: making a commitment to your legal career; setting goals for your practice; and maintaining perspective.

Making a Commitment

Above all, in order to be a successful attorney, you must make a decided mental commitment to your career. You have to be com-

TIP

You either want to succeed or you don't. If you do, making an express mental commitment to your practice is an important step in the process.

mitted to your daily work and to the present moment. This commitment always has to be at the forefront of your mind.

You have probably heard your law school classmates or new colleagues comment that they accepted a position as an associate in a top-tier law firm solely to pay off student loans. Or maybe they accepted a position as a clerk in a solo practitioner's office only temporarily, until a more lucrative position presents itself. These are classic examples of not making a commitment, and this is always a big mistake.

No matter what job you get out of law school, you have to be committed to it. You have to be present not only physically but mentally, too. Coming out of law school, many years ago now, Kevin had an offer with a firm that paid well and another offer with attorneys who were going to pay him much less but who had a reputation for being nice. He chose the nice guys. He worked hard, invested himself in his practice, and never looked back at the money he left on the table. Now he is one of the name partners of that firm and one of the most successful trial attorneys in Chicago.

Not everyone's story will be exactly like this, of course. Regardless, though, if you want a shot, you must be committed. The truth is, you have no idea where your first, second, third, and so on jobs out of law school will take you. You don't know who you are going to meet along the way. None of us do. The job that you regard as temporary just might open a door for you or present an opportunity that you could never have imagined.

If you are not committed to your practice, you will miss incredible opportunities. If you are not committed, the sacrifices that you will inevitably be called upon to make as a new lawyer will not seem worth it. If your mind-set is that your career is a temporary one, it will be. When you are not committed to your practice, you are, simply, not being the best practitioner that you can be.

TIP

Set express, concrete, written goals for your practice each year.

Setting Goals

In addition to making a commitment, setting goals is absolutely critical to your success as an attorney. There is no way around this. In fact, to be successful at anything, you must set express, concrete, written goals and an action plan in furtherance of those goals.

I have observed that some new lawyers go into a law firm thinking that their careers and the direction of their careers somehow belong to someone else. They assume that if they show up every day, keep their heads down, and do their work, someone will pluck them from the rest of the associate pool and move them forward. They assume that, with this passive approach, they might wake up one day and find themselves as managing partners of the law firm. No. Sorry. This is not how it works.

In reality, no one is looking out for your career. No one but you can steer the course of your career. You will likely have mentors and advisers and, over time, people in the firm advocating for your success. This is not the same, though, as putting mechanisms in place year after year to ensure that you are taking charge of your own fate by setting realistic goals and achieving those goals. This responsibility falls on you. Be proactive. Seek out work that is meaningful to you and that will further your career. Do pro bono work and work on smaller matters in order to accelerate your experience. Take matters into your own hands.

Here is my advice for crafting goals and a personalized action plan: take it year by year (your objective as soon as you have finished this book is to set your goals for this upcoming year!). Identify two to three "big goals" for the year and craft a specific action plan in furtherance of those goals. Devise crystal-clear goals and then break down the small actions that will lead to achieving them. Calendar these actions and implement them throughout the year, ensuring that you accomplish your goals before the year ends.

TIP

If you are uncertain of what is a realistic goal for an associate at your level, sit down with a mentor or senior attorney and seek some guidance about goals for your practice. They will welcome this and think highly of the fact that you are making the effort.

As an example, a big goal for a junior litigation associate may be to take a deposition. The actions throughout the year that will lead to this include: sharing with your mentor and the attorneys in your department that you would be interested in taking a minor deposition if the opportunity presents itself (calendar this for January); participating in deposition training or in-house workshops (February and March); accompanying attorneys in your office on depositions to observe how they take depositions, even if it means that you don't bill your time for it (April and May); helping several attorneys prepare for their own depositions by creating deposition outlines, organizing documents, and thinking strategically about the global objectives of each deposition (June and July); and working with an assistant to coordinate deposition logistics for an upcoming deposition (August). By fall, you will have positioned yourself to accomplish the goal of taking a deposition.

Maintaining Perspective

Finally, you will be well served by maintaining perspective throughout the course of your career. Although it is important that you are dedicated to your practice and serious about the work that you are doing, in the end, this is just a job. It is bigger and more important than that in a lot of ways, but it is a job, a profession, a way to make a living. How you approach your job can certainly say something about the kind of person you are, but it should not be the only thing of value in your life. Take pride in being an attorney, but revel in things outside of work as well. And remember that no matter what happens, if you have done your very best, if you have given your all, you will nearly always be fine.

4

YOUR ROLE IN A LAW FIRM

This is completely counterintuitive, but unless you are reading this book, no one is going to tell you what your role is as a new lawyer in a law firm. This makes no sense, I know, but it is a fact. The senior lawyers and administrators in most law firms assume that you will just figure it out eventually. And you will, but this is a horrible business model. How can you be expected to do your job (much less do your job well) if you are not told what it is?

In any event, a law firm associate plays a number of key roles. Most importantly, you are to act as support staff for more senior attorneys, generate a profit, and service firm clients. The sooner you assume these

TIP

As a new lawyer in a law firm, your role, above all, is to act as part of a larger support staff for more senior attorneys.

roles, the sooner you will become an indispensable member of the firm as a whole.

Acting as Support Staff for More Senior Attorneys

The best way to think about your role in a law firm in the early years of your practice is as a supportive one. Your role is to act as support staff for the more senior attorneys in your office. I fought this quite a bit in my early practice—I wanted to matter so much more than that. However, demonstrating that you understand this role and actually providing a foundation of support for the attorneys with whom you are working is a great way to accelerate your career and position yourself as a superstar associate.

Depending on the size of the firm, your workload and the nature of your work will vary significantly. In a larger firm, your primary roles may be to review documents and proofread or input handwritten changes into a document. In a smaller firm, you may be running cases or deals from day one. No matter the size of your firm and the depth of your work, your role is going to be a supportive one. You are there to assist the senior attorneys in accomplishing client work, and you are there to make them look good.

Think of this as you approach each task. Have you taken on as much responsibility as you can? Have you taken ownership of the work that you have been assigned? Have you given the best support that you can give?

Generating a Profit

Another distinct role of any lawyer in a law firm environment is to generate a profit. This is one of the most basic principles of the business world, but, as lawyers, we tend to forget this. The theoretical nature of law school leads us to believe that we are immune from this somehow—that there is some intrinsic value in just pontificating about the law (and there is some, but this is not a moneymaking proposition, I can assure you).

Before we talk about profitability, let's take a moment to consider law firm salaries. Most associates are salaried employees, though this salary will vary quite a bit from practice to practice, from city to city, and from small to midsize to large law firm. Compensation is largely driven by the market and the firm's financial status and expenses. From year to year, depending on performance and (again) the firm's financial status and expenses, you may also be eligible for a salary increase and midyear or year-end bonuses as well.

> **TIP**
> Law firms are businesses, plain and simple, and being mindful of profitability as a new lawyer is going to set you apart.

Now, the question of profitability depends largely on the type of firm you join. If you are required to bill hours, that is, attribute your working time to specific clients, your goal is to meet your target hours (generally speaking, this will be in the range of 1,800 to 2,000 hours per year) in an efficient manner. (We will talk more later about billing time.) The best way to do this is to maximize your working time, or "utilization rate." In other words, for every hour you are at the firm,

TIP

In the early years of your practice, you have two sets of clients: the more senior attorneys who are giving you work and the clients who have hired the firm to do legal work on their behalf.

in an ideal world, you should bill a client for that hour. Of course, this is not entirely realistic: in a typical working day, you will engage in many nonbillable tasks, including chatting with your colleagues, eating lunch, and taking a coffee break. However, it is helpful to keep in mind that both your billable hours and your utilization rate bear on profitability.

If you are not required to bill hours (e.g., if you are working for a plaintiffs' firm or in an area of law where work is charged at a flat rate), your profitability is determined by subtracting your salary plus yearly benefits from the amount of money you bring to the firm. As an easy example, let's say you make $45,000 as an associate in a boutique plaintiffs' firm that is paid in contingency fees. Your yearly benefits amount to $5,000 for the firm. Throughout the course of your first year, you handle three small cases each worth $100,000. You win two of the three. The firm collects approximately $33,000 from each of the two cases you won (a one-third contingency fee is traditional in plaintiffs' firms), for a total of $66,000. In this example, you have proven to be a profitable associate because you have brought in $16,000 over and above your salary plus yearly benefits of $50,000.

Although your objective in the early years of your practice is to learn your practice area, demonstrate that you are a superstar associate, and, as previously discussed, act as support staff for more senior attorneys, your awareness of your own profitability will make you that much more compelling as a member of the firm.

Servicing Clients

Finally, your role as a law firm associate is to service clients. Again, this is something that lawyers tend to forget in the early years of their practice, but it is critical. Law firms exist solely to service clients. And you, in turn, exist to do the same.

When I first started practicing, I was advised to think of myself as a solo practitioner (with all of my overhead and other expenses paid by someone else!). As a solo practitioner, it was my job to bring in "clients" to give me work. Those clients were the more senior attorneys in the office. Every time a senior attorney walks down the halls of the office with an assignment to give out, he is "shopping" for an attorney to do his work. You want that senior attorney to choose you. You want that senior attorney to think of you first as the best lawyer for the job. To ensure that this happens, you must do good work again and again (and we'll talk about how to do this shortly).

In addition to making the more senior attorneys happy, your work has to be of value for firm clients. Even if you do not have direct contact with clients in the early years of your practice, all of your work is ultimately for the benefit of a client. Keep this in mind as you work. Stay client focused and client driven.

TIP

Consider each project that you take on from the perspective of the client: are you approaching your work in a way that is most beneficial or useful for the client's end goal or purpose?

5

PROFESSIONALISM

Lawyers are professionals. Law school is, by definition, a professional school, and it is meant to produce professionals. (If your law school experience was anything like mine—bar parties and sweatpants—this likely comes as a complete surprise.) Joining your firm, you will be expected to act like a professional. And acting like a professional is an important way to get ahead.

You can demonstrate that you are a professional in a number of ways. Your attire, demeanor, and interpersonal skills all bear on your professionalism.

Attire

As simple as it may seem, the way you dress in a corporate environment is exceedingly important. This is the very first impression you make.

If your workplace observes a business dress code or for any formal business occasions (e.g., client meetings, court hearings, or depositions), wear a suit. As a rule of thumb, when in doubt, wear a suit. You will never be accused of being overdressed in a law firm environment (well, almost never: you may work for a sporting goods client—I'll explain later).

If your office observes a business casual dress code, this calls for something slightly less formal than a suit. Still, your attire should be traditional and conservative. For men, slacks, a tucked-in collared shirt, and a sweater or sport coat in the cooler months are typical. For women, slacks, knee-length skirts, conservative dresses, collared shirts, and cardigans are typical. Flashy, quirky, or otherwise inappropriate attire is never well received in a professional environment.

If you are meeting with foreign clients (or with clients who have any particularities or nuances), research the proper dress code in advance or ask someone who has previously worked with the client.

TIP

Although in the early years you may not know exactly what you are doing in your substantive practice, acting in a professional manner at all times and in all instances is completely in your control and absolutely mandatory.

Certain cultures have more stringent ideas about professional attire, and certain companies have their own unique dress codes and preferences.

As an example, a team of attorneys at my law firm met with a national outdoor gear and sporting goods company (I told you I'd come back to this!). As is customary, the lawyers went dressed in suits. After the meeting, which I understand went very well, the general counsel of the company told our lawyers that they should not wear suits to their offices going forward. The suits were out of place. The company representatives, across the board, were wearing cargo shorts and T-shirts.

TIP
Keep a clean, pressed suit hanging behind your door or neatly folded in your cubicle so you always have a suit on hand if you need one.

It is also important to put thought into your attire for law firm functions outside of the office. At casual firm functions, such as a baseball game in the firm box or a happy hour with lawyers from the antitrust group, dress nicely and dress conservatively even though you are dressed down. Khakis, a collared shirt, and a sport coat or blazer are an easy go-to for both men and women.

For a more upscale firm function outside of the office, such as a firm dinner or charity event, dressy conservative attire is your safest bet. Risqué, unusual, cutting-edge, or otherwise revealing attire is never a good idea.

As a related matter, on your commute to and from work, it is acceptable to opt for comfortable shoes. Still, be mindful of your choice

TIP

In addition to looking like a professional, you want to be communicative and impressive throughout the duration of any firm event. So, err on the side of drinking a minimal amount of alcohol. A good rule of thumb is one drink and two glasses of water every two hours. (If this sounds like a drag to you, please feel free to go home and down a bottle of wine. Just don't do it in front of the people who sign your paychecks.) And don't drink excessively just because others are doing it. You don't know what reputations they have or what repercussions they will face as a result.

of footwear. Buy shoes that are comfortable but stylish, and preferably all black. The shoes should be closed toe (never flip-flops!). If you live in a place where it snows, find a reasonable (not ludicrous) pair of snow boots. Change your shoes before you get to your office (and preferably not in a public area). This whole shoe discussion might sound a bit crazy, but it's actually the bane of many partners' existence: year after year, they see new lawyers whom they perceive as unprofessional largely because they are bumming around the office in flip-flops or gigantic, fluffy snow boots. At bottom, it's a waste of an opportunity.

When you dress like a professional, your colleagues will assume that you are a professional. A sloppy, indifferent, or otherwise inappropriate look, on the other hand, suggests that you practice in an equally careless manner.

Demeanor

Much like attire, mastering the proper demeanor in a professional environment will be central to your success.

In your practice, take care to act in a formal, professional manner. With this said, you also want to approach your office interactions in a relaxed, natural way. Your demeanor should reflect that you are serious about your work but that you are also an open, friendly person. If you can demonstrate by your demeanor that you are both of these things, your colleagues will respect you and want to work with you. You will also be selected first to participate in client meetings and pitches for new business.

Finally, as a new lawyer, you will be well served by expressing enthusiasm at the prospect of working on any case, deal, or project that comes across your desk. (I'm going to reiterate this part about enthusiasm in a moment because it's that important.) You should be genuinely curious about the work you are given, and you should be excited to take it on.

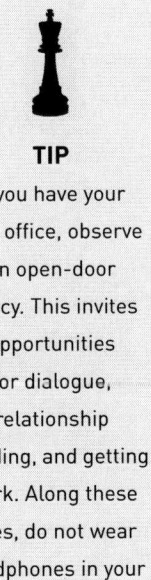

TIP

If you have your own office, observe an open-door policy. This invites opportunities for dialogue, relationship building, and getting work. Along these lines, do not wear headphones in your office. More senior attorneys in your law firm may regard this as dismissive, unfriendly, or flippant behavior.

Interpersonal Skills

Finding success in a professional environment depends in large part on capitalizing on your own personal strengths and minimizing your weaknesses. In a legal environment, in particular, where you are expected to work closely with colleagues and clients day after day and for long hours, honing your interpersonal skills is a must.

Although not everyone has the same interpersonal qualities, there are a few rules to live by:

TIP
Enthusiastic lawyers are more pleasant to work with and in turn get more work.

Be reasonable and even tempered at all times. Do not display extreme emotions, and do not take frustrations out on anyone (this includes your administrative assistant—the best way to get in trouble as a new lawyer is to treat staff in a disrespectful manner).

Be enthusiastic. Express enthusiasm at the prospect of working on any project assigned to you.

Get to know your colleagues. Ask them about their work and their interests.

Be humble. You are at the bottom of the food chain. Your likability, and not your credentials (even if impressive), is going to carry the day.

Steer clear of office gossip or any office dynamics with which you are not comfortable. Use discretion, and keep your personal drama out of the workplace.

Do not take things personally. You are there to do a job. Period. Do not view minor exchanges or critiques of your work as personal affronts. Criticism in particular is expected, and you should use it to improve your skills.

Demonstrate that you are a reliable person. Act responsibly and responsively. Always do what you say you are going to do when you say you are going to do it; even if you have promised to do something that is ultimately insignificant, you will build credibility by consistently doing exactly what you say you are going to do. Be on time; better yet, be early—for everything. Do your work quickly, efficiently, and with purpose. Where appropriate, keep your supervising attorney apprised of your progress.

Work hard. Early in your career, demonstrate that you are willing to put in long hours and late nights. Volunteer to take over or help out on projects and cases wherever you might be needed. Figure out how to get work done quickly, efficiently, and well. Create strategies for limiting distractions throughout the day. Where necessary to get work done, turn your e-mail alerts off and make conversations with people in the office short. In other words, show that you mean business most of the time.

Be mindful of generational differences. Attorneys are retiring later and later in their careers and new lawyers are often hired in their mid- to late twenties. As a result, there is literally a sixty-year age difference between the oldest and youngest attorneys in many offices. A single office might easily include WWII "Greatest Generation" veterans and Facebook-raised Millennials. As a new lawyer, it is your job to negotiate this difference and make the more senior attorneys feel comfortable interacting with you.

TIP
The best attorneys in any law firm have an impeccable work ethic.

TIP
As an overarching rule, employ good judgment in every situation, even if you have to step back or seek guidance to identify exactly what that good judgment might be.

The best way to approach the senior attorneys in your firm is to treat them with exceeding respect. A deferential demeanor will resonate significantly. Beyond this, use common sense. Work with more senior attorneys in ways that appear most comfortable to them. Opt for face-to-face meetings instead of e-mail correspondence. Assist with typing documents or inputting their handwritten changes into collaborative documents. In all cases, listen and learn from seasoned attorneys. This is a quick way to accelerate your understanding of substantive legal practice. And senior attorneys universally love telling war stories—legal and actual!

6

LITIGATION VERSUS TRANSACTIONAL PRACTICE

Now that we are in the proper frame of mind and somewhat oriented as to our role in a law firm and how to act in a professional manner, let's transition into a discussion of your practice area choice. Your early practice area choice—one of the first decisions that you will make in your professional career—will dictate the course of your entire career going forward. If you think about it, this is completely crazy. Coming out of law school, it is genuinely difficult for lawyers to have clarity or purpose in choosing their practice area. It's certainly hard to appreciate the significance of choosing one practice area over another.

TIP

Consider the implications of choosing a litigation or transactional practice. What kind of work will you be doing? What type of lifestyle will you have? Does this choice comport with your vision of your life as a whole?

The decision is often informed by law school experiences that are designed to mimic an actual legal practice (e.g., moot court or mock negotiations). These law school experiences, while valuable, tend to be tailored to litigation practices and are not sufficient, in and of themselves, to inform your legal practice choice. The experiences are not diagnostic anyway.

Instead, a good way to choose a practice area is to look ahead at the implications of that choice. (And if you have already decided on your practice area, understanding the implications will help you manage expectations and get your bearings sooner.) For example, as a litigator, no matter what your particular focus, you will be expected to have strong legal writing, legal reasoning, and advocacy skills. Over the course of your career, you will write; make court appearances; take and defend depositions; engage in intensive discourse with opposing counsel in formal and informal settings; and, on occasion, try cases.

But there's a lot more to being a litigator, actually. The most successful litigators have unique interpersonal skills and social thresholds: successful litigators love competition; are calm in the face of confrontation; can think and perform on their feet; and, above all, enjoy convincing others daily of their beliefs, positions, and opinions. Good litigators do not take things personally and are invigorated even by small victories.

As a litigator, opportunities to transition to an in-house position with a corporation are few and far between. These positions are highly sought after and thus competitive. With exceptions, if you begin your career as a litigator, you will most likely remain a litigator in some capacity for the duration of your career.

TIP

Litigators are motivated by competition, confrontation, and a desire to win.

Transactional attorneys review and modify documents, craft solutions for clients with diverse business needs, and negotiate tactically. Over the course of a transactional career, attorneys may facilitate corporate mergers and acquisitions, structure other types of financial deals, and further the interests of corporate clients. Given their extensive business knowledge and the managerial nature of their practice, transactional attorneys often transition to in-house positions. If your objective is ultimately to work for a corporation, whether as legal counsel or as an executive, you would do well to choose a transactional practice area, regardless of your other skills.

TIP

Transactional attorneys are diligent and precise, and, over time, master the art of negotiation and compromise.

There are hundreds of other, more specific legal specializations—some of which do not fall neatly on either side of the transactional/litigation divide. Whatever type of practice you intend to pursue, it is useful to meet with experienced attorneys in that practice area before you make your commitment. You may want to ask them how busy they have been over the past several years and if they have noticed a trend in the need for lawyers with that specialization. You may also ask them if there are other career opportunities available for attorneys in that practice area. Down the road, these will be things that will affect your life directly. You will always want to have a healthy workload and many career options.

As an aside, after a year or two of practice in a firm, it is uncommon (though not impossible) to change practice areas. This is due in large part to the formative nature of those early years of your legal practice. A law firm generally is not going to place a fifth-year and (relatively) experienced litigator as a first-year in the corporate department, for example—and if it did so, this would likely impact the attorney's salary and promotion track.

7

LAW FIRM STRUCTURE

If you ran your own business, you would likely know every last detail about the way the business was structured. Knowing this information minimizes risk, maximizes profit, and increases productivity, among other things.

You should approach your career in a law firm in a similar manner. Learn how your law firm is structured. Understand your position within that structure and how to move your career forward. (If this information is not readily available or otherwise made known to associates, seek out the information from practice area coordinators, mentors, and associate liaisons.) In your time at the

TIP
From day one, invest yourself in your law firm as if you had a personal stake or interest in the firm.

firm, whether it is six months or sixty years, approach your work every day as if you were an owner in the business. And one day you will be.

Firms: Size and Corresponding Structure

In a small firm, the structure is often apparent on its face. Typically, there are a handful of partners and a handful of associates working together in a traditional partnership setting. It is clear who the partners are and who the associates are. If making partner is an option, it is likely based on a subjective combination of your ability to do good work and bring in business.

In traditional midsize to large firms, the structure tends to be more defined. Presently, most firms are structured as limited liability partnerships, and there are a number of attorney designations within that partnership.

Attorney Designations

Associate and Ancillary Positions

"Junior associates" are a law firm's newest hires. First- to third-year associates typically fall into the category of junior associates. Law firms generally invest a lot of money in junior associates by paying them high salaries despite their general lack of skills, with the hope that these associates will be loyal to the firm and, in a best-case scenario, become the managing partners of the firm down the line. The salaries for junior associates vary widely from firm to firm and from city to city. In good economic times, law firms may offer performance-based midyear and year-end bonuses in addition to salary.

Fourth- to sixth-year associates are considered "midlevel associates." Midlevel associates are more comfortable than junior associates with daily practice and can generally handle substantive tasks without excessive instruction and supervision. Midlevel associates who show initiative, take ownership of their work (more about this later), and seek out advanced projects will likely progress more quickly than their peers.

"Senior associates" are often the most sought-after attorneys in a law firm. Seventh-year associates and above are generally classified as senior associates; in some firms, particularly on the East Coast, it is not unusual for attorneys to be associates for a decade or more of practice. Senior associates are experienced, capable attorneys who can handle substantive work with little supervision but can also be billed to clients at reasonable rates (more to come on billing rates, profitability, and time entries shortly). Making it seven plus years in a firm says something about your dedication to the firm and to your practice. Chances are, if you have made it this long, you are a valued associate.

Thus far, we've talked about associate positions up the chain. Let's deviate for a moment and talk about a few ancillary law firm positions. "Of counsel" or "counsel" attorneys are typically more senior than the senior associates but for one reason or another are not on a traditional partnership track. Attorneys may choose an of counsel path if they are working part-time, have not developed sufficient business relative to their years at the firm, or are otherwise not quite ready for partnership. For more senior attorneys who have not been made partner, the title *of counsel* may help generate business and project to the external world that they are beyond associate level. (Very senior partners who are transitioning out of partnership status but still want to act as advisers to the firm are often given the *of counsel* designation as well.)

"Contract attorneys" are typically hired for a discreet project or case where the firm's internal personnel cannot or should not be handling the work that needs to be done. Using contract attorneys can be cost-effective and efficient. However, contract attorneys typically are not hired as full-blown associates once the specific project or case is complete; generally speaking, acting as a contract attorney is not a way to get your foot in the door of a law firm, though it is good exposure to law firm work and generally pays well, too.

Partner Positions

Beyond associate (and related) attorneys, midsize to large law firms are made up of "partners." Firms typically have either a one- or a two-tiered partnership system.

In a one-tiered partnership system, senior associates who have performed exceptionally well over the course of seven, eight, or nine years (or sometimes longer) are promoted to partner. In a one-tiered system, once you are made partner, you have reached the highest designation in the firm. However, many law firms with a one-tiered partnership system have levels within the tier that separate the experienced partners with big books of business from the newly appointed partners who likely do not have much, if any, business of their own, and compensation differs on each level within the tier.

In a two-tiered partnership system, senior associates who have performed exceptionally well over the course of seven, eight, or nine years (or sometimes longer) are promoted to "income partner." Typically, income partners do not share in the equity, or profits, of the firm. Rather, much like associates, income partners are salaried, at-will employees paid slightly more than senior associates, often with the potential to receive midyear and year-end bonuses.

Although the promotion to income partner itself does not result in much of a change for the lawyer within the firm, acquiring the title of *partner* is a symbol of the firm's regard for an attorney's performance up to that point and is also intended to help the attorney generate business, an important aspect of being a partner. Prospective clients are more likely to engage in discussions with a partner in a law firm about their legal needs than to engage in such discussions with an associate.

TIP
To the outside world, an income partner is simply a partner—in other words, the distinction is for internal purposes only, and income partners may represent to the world that they are partners in the firm.

Despite the benefits of being promoted to income partner, there is an unexpected nuance to think about: income partners are billed to clients at fairly high rates, which can sometimes result in a reduction in the amount of work that more senior partners are willing to assign to income partners. Some clients would prefer not to have two partners billing on their files, and, as previously discussed, senior associates are often capable of doing the very same work at lower rates. This is one downside in the early years of making partner in a firm.

"Contract partners" (distinguished from contract attorneys, previously discussed) are partners who are employed by the firm under a specific employment contract that generally has a term of years and specifies a minimum amount of compensation for the partner. Often, lateral partners (partners who come from another firm) start as contract partners for a specific number of years, thus allowing the firm to comply with common partner agreements that specify that attorneys must be with the firm for a certain minimum number of years before they can be an equity partner. As with income partners, the *contract partner* designation is generally not identified outside the firm and may even be unknown to all but the firm's equity partners.

Finally, in midsize to large law firms, "equity partner" is the highest level you can achieve. Typically, an equity partner will have to "buy into" the firm, much like purchasing stock in a corporation. The amount of equity buy-in varies by firm but can easily exceed $100,000, though often the buy-in can be made over several years. Although equity partners share in the profits, or equity, of the firm, their portion of the share is typically proportionate in some way to the amount of business they bring into the firm. An equity partner's compensation may vary significantly from year to year; and, as you might expect, an equity partner shares in the losses of the firm, if any, as well.

An equity partner's primary responsibility is to generate value for the firm. Although an equity partner is also required to oversee and work on complex cases, handle administrative issues, and manage client relations, the ability to generate business is often the key to the success of an equity partner. Many law firm partners will tell you that the only way to have any security in private practice is to have clients of your own. In most firms equity partners who bring in clients for other partners and associates to service receive credits (or shares) for the hours billed to those clients without having to do the actual work.

TIP
Learn your firm's written and unwritten criteria for each step in the progression from associate to partner.

This is a key concept in understanding the dynamic in a law firm, so an example is in order: A high-level intellectual property (IP) attorney at a large, full-service law firm is friendly with the chief executive officer (CEO) of a former Fortune 500 company. The Fortune 500 company is now embroiled in a complex bankruptcy matter. The IP attorney tells the CEO that his firm has an outstanding bankruptcy department, and the CEO agrees to hire the IP attorney's firm. The IP attorney has now brought a large, complex bankruptcy matter into the firm that will be handled exclusively by the bankruptcy department. The IP attorney is not even qualified to work on the bankruptcy matter. Still, he will get credit—which, in turn, results in compensation—for the work done and hours billed by the bankruptcy attorneys. His income, with respect to this case anyway, is passive (the best kind!).

Getting from Point A to Point B

As a final point, it is worthwhile as an associate to understand how and why your firm promotes certain attorneys. Although every law firm is different, certain qualities will always serve you well on the path from associate to partner. Among others, exhibiting hard work and dedication; taking a holistic approach to the cases, projects, or deals that you are assigned; and demonstrating that you are invested in the firm by volunteering for committees, internal publications, and client pitches will say a lot about your drive to move up the ladder.

Above all, understanding what your specific firm expects of its lawyers will be key to actually delivering on that expectation and getting ahead. You should understand how your firm assigns credit for client matters, too, since business credit in a law firm is, generally speaking, king. Often credit can be divided in some manner between the partners or associates who bring a client into the firm (e.g., our IP attorney) and the partners or associates who are responsible for actually overseeing and working on the particular matter (e.g., our bankruptcy attorneys).

8

MENTORSHIP

In a law firm, there is a special value or significance in the word *mentor*. If you choose the right mentor, that person will be like family, and your life will be better for it.

Finding a mentor is one of the most important things that you will do in your career. Professionals with strong mentors and career advisers have higher job satisfaction and a greater likelihood of success in their careers. And securing strong mentoring relationships early on in your career can help you master many of the personal and professional skills we are discussing here.

Many firms have a formal mentoring program in place. You

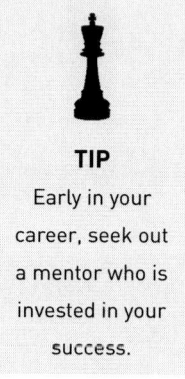

TIP

Early in your career, seek out a mentor who is invested in your success.

may be assigned to a mentor in the first days or weeks at the firm. In some instances, this pairing works perfectly. If so, great. Other times, it is not ideal because the person did not necessarily volunteer to be your mentor, and the connection or camaraderie may be tenuous. The assigned mentor may not be interested in taking on the type of mentorship role we are talking about here. If you are assigned a mentor whom you feel is not an ideal one, develop a relationship with that person anyway (the more relationships you build the better) but also look for additional mentors who are better suited for you.

Over the course of your career, it is a good idea to have several mentors, each of whom can contribute something unique to your career development. Choose your first mentor early in your career in order to gain from the benefits of mentorship right away (and strive to be that mentor for someone else down the line).

Given the significance of mentorship, you should be discerning and selective in choosing your mentor. In choosing your mentor, keep the following in mind:

Choose someone internal. Your mentor should be someone internal (not your uncle who is a lawyer in the Cayman Islands). Your mentor should be in a position to help you decipher and navigate your specific office dynamics.

Choose someone in your practice group. Choosing a mentor in your specific practice group will ensure that your mentor can help you on a day-to-day basis with any substantive questions you may have. Your mentor may also prove to be a good source of work when things are slow.

Choose someone who is trustworthy. From time to time, you will have to rely on your mentor to help you negotiate sensitive issues, whether personal or related to legal practice. Your mentor must be someone whom you can trust. Although trust is a difficult thing to gauge at first, seek out someone who does not gossip or speak badly of others. This is the type of mentor who will also keep *your* confidences.

Choose someone who is sociable. The best mentors are sociable and well liked in your office. An outsider likely will not be in a good position to help you understand and integrate into your firm or other legal practice.

Choose someone who is reasonably busy. Although this may sound counterintuitive, you want a mentor who is well regarded from a work standpoint. In addition, as mentioned above, a busy mentor will prove to be a good source of work. (Of course, whether your mentor is busy or not, be mindful, respectful, and appreciative of your mentor's time.)

Choose someone who has been at your office five or more years. It is important that your mentor actually understand your substantive legal practice as well as the office in which you practice. In fewer than five years, it is difficult to have a comprehensive understanding of either of these things.

9

TIME MANAGEMENT AND ORGANIZATION

In creating rubrics and methodologies for teaching time management and organizational skills, I have learned that these skills are hyperpersonal and tend to be acquired over time. If you have not worked in a corporate environment before, managing multiple projects and meeting multiple and competing deadlines are among the first things that you will have to master. The sooner you can figure out a system that works for you, the sooner you will get work done effectively and efficiently. We will discuss some foundational concepts here that will get you started.

TIP

As you are planning your days, anticipate delays. Build in time for any unexpected delays. As a new lawyer, everything takes longer than expected. Aim to get all of your work done well in advance of the big deadlines you have calendared. Do not allow yourself to wait until the last minute to do anything.

Time Management

Importance of Time Management

A typical day in a law firm begins anywhere between 7:30 a.m. and 9:30 a.m. (this is largely city- or practice group–dependent: New York lawyers, for example, are notorious for a late start time, as are corporate attorneys). Early in your career, err on the side of starting your day early. You will inevitably need more time to get your work done than the attorneys around you, and you will impress your colleagues by being the first one in the office in the morning.

As a law firm associate, your day, for the most part, is your own. You have to get your work done according to any and all deadlines; but, within the time frame of your deadlines, you can choose to do your work in any manner you would like. (Of course, if you are working closely with more senior attorneys, your schedule, at a minimum, should mimic theirs.)

Your work will vary significantly depending on your practice area, but you should expect to do certain things as a junior associate regardless of your substantive area of focus. These things include: responding to e-mails (sometimes hundreds a day); editing; cite checking and proofreading documents; researching case law, statutes, and corporate filings; attending meetings (internal and external); and speaking with colleagues, clients, and opposing counsel.

An effective way to manage your time from day to day is to sketch out two-week periods at a time. Calendar the big items (any formal and informal deadlines) you have to get done in that two-week period, and then fill in your calendar with all of the daily items you will need to do to be sure the big items get done on time. Use this two-week calendar as a checklist. Set reminders and check your calendar daily to be sure that nothing is overlooked. As new deadlines emerge, add those to your two-week calendar.

As an aside, whether you use an electronic calendar or a handwritten calendar is simply a matter of preference. I always use both. The act of handwriting my daily tasks helps me process what I have to do. Inputting tasks into the electronic calendar allows me to set electronic reminders and share calendar dates as relevant with colleagues.

TIP

Fill your daily working calendar in two-week intervals. Identify the big items as well as the daily work that will have to be done to fulfill the big items. Each day you should revisit your calendar and fill in one more day at the back end of the two-week period.

Whatever you choose, I encourage you to learn how your firm's electronic calendaring system works. You will want to use the communal calendar to keep track of deadlines for the cases, projects, or

TIP
Show initiative through your management and organization of the master calendar for each case, project, or deal that you are working on.

deals that you are working on. If you are working with more senior attorneys, take initiative with the communal calendar. As soon as a relevant date or deadline is announced, put it on the calendars of all of the people working on the case, project, or deal. One of my colleagues made a name for herself in the firm by acting hyperresponsibly and overseeing the master calendar for every case that she was working on. Because she was doing it, the more senior attorneys did not have to, which made their jobs—and lives—easier.

A typical day in a law firm ends anywhere between 6:00 p.m. and 7:30 p.m., depending on your workload. During busy periods, expect to stay much later. In all cases, do not leave unless all of your work for that day is complete.

Time Management Tips

If you struggle with working independently or managing time in an unstructured environment, consider the following tips:

Get work done systematically. When we have a lot to do, as everyone does each and every day, we tend to dabble. We open one project, start another, take a phone call. Instead of making small dents in all of your work, get your work done systematically. Carve out three hours to start and finish a project before you move on to the next one. Tackle your projects in order of priority first and then in order of how quickly you can accomplish the project. (With this said, you don't want to rush—make sure you are taking the time to do all of your work well.) The more you can cross off your list each day, the better.

Get help. Whether you work with a personal administrative assistant, a firm-wide assistant, or a paralegal, figure out how to ask for and get help when you need it. Have clarity about the tasks for which you are solely responsible and the tasks that you can pass along. Delegate and get back to work.

Turn off e-mail alerts. Instead of checking your e-mail every three minutes or every time you are notified that a new e-mail has come in, check your e-mail on a regular schedule and turn off your e-mail alerts during the day. The fewer distractions you have, the more likely you are to get to the items on your checklist.

Stay off of social media sites, blogs, etc. There is a lot of business value in the information contained on the Internet. However, surfing the Internet aimlessly is a time suck and in no way furthers your goal of getting work done quickly and efficiently. As with e-mail, if you are on sites like Twitter or LinkedIn or Facebook for work purposes (we will discuss some good reasons for this shortly), create a systematic time and place for checking those sites, and then forget about them until evening or the following day.

Organization
Importance of Organization

As a rule, lawyers have horrible organizational skills, which, if you are paranoid about professional responsibility, is bad news. At the risk of sounding dramatic, a disorganized practice is a malpractice action waiting to happen. In any event, it is so much harder to practice law when you are disorganized. If you start your practice with a definitive plan for staying organized, it will eventually become a habit.

Organization Tips
Office Organization

An organized practice starts with an organized office. This is simple, but it's key. If your office is organized, you will have a better handle on your work and you will minimize the possibility of overlooking something important.

There are a number of things that you can do to keep your office organized:

Clear your desktop. Your desktop should have only the essentials: a computer, a telephone, a designated legal pad and pen for taking telephone messages, and a penholder. All other supplies should be kept neatly in a desk drawer labeled "Supplies."

Go paperless. Where possible, keep the paper in your office to a minimum. Think before you print. For any hard-copy document, make a decision about what you are going to do with the document as soon as you receive it. Your options are keeping it available for reference, filing it, or shredding it. Of course, before you shred any documents or delete any e-mails, be sure that you are crystal-clear on your firm's document-retention and document-deletion policies and that you are strictly following those policies.

Clear the floor. The floor of your office should be free of books,

TIP

A messy office leaves a bad impression on colleagues and clients. It suggests that your practice is similarly out of sorts.

papers, and files. Think fire department–approved. Use shelves, clearly marked boxes, and drawers instead.

Organize nightly and weekly. Take five minutes at the end of each day to straighten up your office. This makes for a more palatable working environment the next morning. And designate one morning a week (as a suggestion, use Fridays—they tend to be slow days anyway) to reorganizing your office as necessary.

Substantive Practice Organization

In addition to keeping your office organized, you should keep an organized substantive practice. You'll see frantic lawyers running to court with stained suits, untied shoes, and overstuffed files spilling out of their arms. This is alarming. Let's not do that.

There are several key ways to keep your substantive practice organized:

Hoard legal pads. Seriously. You can never have too many. Keep a separate legal pad for each case, project, or deal that you are working on. Designate the case, project, or deal on the cover of the legal pad. Do not combine notes from any other cases, projects, or deals. The idea behind this is simple: you want the quickest, most efficient access to information. If a partner comes into your office and asks to see your notes from the meeting last week on X case and you have to frantically flip through five different legal pads to find what the partner is looking for (while making small talk to kill the time), you will come across as a lunatic. And disorganized.

File, label, repeat. For all hard copies in your office, use files and labels to sort and organize. The only files out should be files of pending cases, projects, or deals. Everything else should be filed away in drawers or long-term storage. All files and subfiles should have clear labels (e.g., file: Jones v. Smith; subfile 1: Research; subfile 2: Drafts; subfile 3: Legal Pads, etc.). As with legal pads, keep a separate working file for each case, project, or deal that you are working on.

Make lists. Your practice should be organized by lists. Keep a list of all of your current projects taped to your desk. Keep a list of key telephone numbers by your phone. Keep a list of your firm-related passwords on a sticky note on your computer (you probably don't want display your personal passwords, but keep available any passwords for sites you regularly visit to do your work, e.g., Lexis). Along the same lines, bookmark any key URLs for your practice.

Organize your e-mail inbox. We are going to get to substantive e-mail writing shortly, but I want to mention a few things here while we're focused on organization. Your professional inbox cannot resemble the personal e-mail account that you abandoned three years ago. E-mail writing comprises so much of what we do as attorneys, and your practice will run more smoothly if you are diligent about keeping your e-mail inbox organized.

As an initial matter, for any case or project that you are assigned, create a corresponding e-mail folder right away. All electronic correspondence for that case or project should go into that folder. For every e-mail that comes to your inbox thereafter, force yourself to do one of three things: delete the e-mail (e.g., if it is spam, unsolicited, or otherwise not intended for you); file the e-mail in its appropriate subfolder; or convert the e-mail into an action plan (if the e-mail calls upon you to respond, follow up, research, etc., calendar this action, get it done, and file the e-mail away once you have done so).

10

WORKING WITH STAFF

If you have not yet begun working in a law firm (or in any legal environment), you are not going to believe me when I say that building relationships with staff members is among the most important things you can do for your early career. But believe me. It's true.

Certain staff members carry more weight and are more important than many of the attorneys in your firm. It is not uncommon in a law firm for staff members to have been with the firm for ten, twenty, or even thirty years, and these staff members are often trusted confidants, practice managers, and friends of the most senior members of the firm. You won't know who they are at first, which makes them that much more powerful.

As a new lawyer in a law firm, you must treat everyone with courtesy and respect. This is truly not negotiable. Let me justify this arguably patronizing statement: year after year, new lawyers are blacklisted (or worse) based on unwarranted, foolish behavior toward law firm staff. Although most of you will never act this way, I'm helping out the few who might let frustration or self-importance get the better of them. Not only should you treat staff members nicely because it is the right thing to do, but also because you cannot afford the potential career repercussions.

TIP

There is a lot to be learned from law firm staff, both substantively and in terms of law firm politics and dynamics.

Administrative Assistants

The Basics

Your relationship with your administrative assistant will be a defining one in your career. If the relationship is strong, it will make a significant difference in the quality and ease of your legal practice. Although you are not required to be best friends with your assistant, at a minimum your goal is to have a streamlined, amicable working relationship so that your days are pleasant and your practice runs smoothly.

Although a good relationship is important, lawyers and administrative assistants do play distinct roles in a law firm setting, and it will be your responsibility to maintain these clearly delineated roles. In theory, administrative assistants work "for" the lawyers to whom they are assigned. Now, this does not mean that you are your assistant's boss in the traditional sense, but you will be in a position to assign work, much like senior lawyers will assign work to you.

In assigning work to your assistant, do so politely and courteously but with confidence and clarity. Assign specific tasks and explain those tasks thoroughly and clearly. Include all key details, deadlines, and other project nuances. If you have specific expectations, share those before your assistant begins the project.

If you share an assistant with other attorneys, be mindful of the hierarchy and of their needs, too. Your work will likely not take priority over a more senior attorney's work. If you have deadlines that are not negotiable, let your assistant know this. If your assistant is unable to help you based on competing assignments from more senior attorneys, arrange to get help elsewhere (e.g., firms often have overflow administrative assistants). Whatever the situation, use your energy wisely. If your assistant has explained that it will be impossible to get to your work in the time frame you need it, there is no sense in arguing or negotiating.

TIP

Do not assume that your administrative assistant can read your mind. You will have to be direct and specific about your expectations. Also, avoid issuing work in question form (e.g., "would it be possible for you to...?"). Simply indicate politely that you have X that needs to be done by X time.

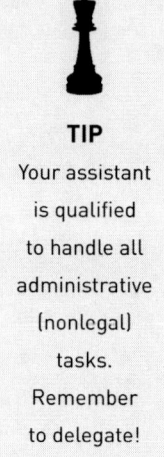

TIP
Your assistant is qualified to handle all administrative (nonlegal) tasks. Remember to delegate!

Be resourceful and go elsewhere. (After the fact, however, if this is a routine occurrence or otherwise complicating your practice, it may be in your best interest to initiate a dialogue with your assistant about this. We will discuss this in more detail shortly.)

So, what type of work should you assign to your administrative assistant? The type of work that an administrative assistant will handle varies from firm to firm; in small and midsize firms, administrative assistants tend to do more substantive work than in larger law firms. As a rule, if your assistant is trained to do a particular task, it is likely proper to assign that task to your assistant.

In most instances, administrative work includes: answering the telephone; taking detailed messages; keeping and organizing files; making photocopies; transmitting documents (via facsimile, e-mail, mail, etc.); submitting reimbursements for expenses; scheduling meetings; creating shell documents; typing handwritten edits into documents; facilitating the completion of projects (e.g., copying final deal binders or court filings); and managing your daily administrative work when you are out of the office.

Some assistants will truly surprise you with their abilities and understanding of the practice of law. Still, an administrative assistant's work is nonlegal. Assistants are not trained as lawyers, and their experience cannot make up for this. Nothing goes out the door (or into the hands of an assigning attorney) without your review and final approval. And any mistakes made by your assistant are yours to assume responsibility for. Period.

In addition to your own assistant, it is a good idea to build strong relationships with the other administrative assistants in your office. You can learn a lot about the attorneys with whom you practice through sociable relationships with their assistants. If your firm has assistants on staff working overnight, it is in your best interest to befriend them, too. You will be amazed at the amount of work that can get done on your behalf while you are sleeping.

Without belaboring this section on administrative assistants, I would be remiss if I didn't mention two additional items: administrative assistant reviews and requests for a change of assistant.

TIP

Give your administrative assistant the benefit of an honest (but tempered) review and show that you have a vested interest in your assistant's success in the firm.

Administrative Assistant Reviews

It is common in law firms to do a yearly or biyearly review of your administrative assistant. Depending on your assistant, this may be a challenge. As difficult as it is, you will be best served by giving an honest evaluation. You should be judicious in your word choice and constructive; giving your assistant an undeservedly glowing review because you fear that your assistant will be hurt, offended, or otherwise upset is not strategic. The objective is to ensure that

TIP
Take a few months to observe your assistant's strengths and weaknesses; based on your observations, devise a specific plan for working together going forward.

you are the best practitioner you can be. In order to accomplish this, your administrative assistant has to fulfill your reasonable expectations.

Until you are in this position, it may be hard to fully understand the dilemma that can arise at review time. By way of illustration, it is not uncommon to work with an administrative assistant who does stellar work for the managing partner of your department but routinely dismisses your work because, frankly, you are not "important" in the sense of the law firm hierarchy. As a new lawyer, you are fearful of giving a negative review because you think it may impact your working relationship with the partner, assistant, or both. And it may. However, as long as you have taken a reasonable, measured position and have concrete items to point to that could be improved upon, the partner will respect this and your assistant will at least be aware that you are serious about your career and expect the assistant to be, too.

Requesting a Change of Assistant

Finally, in your legal practice lifetime, you may find that you have to request a change of assistant. I was in this position as a first-year attorney. It was stressful and time-consuming and not something I would want to go through again.

Requesting a change of administrative assistant is not something that can be taken lightly or done readily. As a rule of thumb, barring extraordinary circumstances, this should be done once in a lifetime. Many seasoned attorneys with whom I have spoken on the topic have suggested that it is not even an option until you have worked with an assistant for a year or more. If after a year and much effort your administrative assistant is repeatedly not meeting your needs and is making your practice more difficult or more stressful than it would be otherwise, arranging for a change may be justified.

Having gone through the process, and given the sensitive nature of it, I have a few suggestions for the best possible approach. The following is a measured, methodical process to ensure that you are handling this correctly:

Keep notes. As soon as you detect a recurring conflict or issue with your assistant, keep notes and other information that will support or evidence the frustrations that you are having. Do this with discretion. Do not manufacture issues or compile petty notes. However, consider keeping notes of work that did not get done or work that was done incorrectly, any relevant e-mail correspondence with your assistant, and other information that will help you move forward in an informed way.

Initiate a conversation. As a first step in resolving any conflict or frustration with your administrative assistant, set up a meeting to speak with your assistant. This should not be a conversation in passing. Designate a fifteen-minute window of time and arrange to speak privately with your assistant. In advance of this meeting, using the notes you have kept, prepare a list of three to five things (no more) that you would like to see done differently. The tone of the meeting should be calm and unemotional. The discussion should center on ways that you and your assistant can work together to do things differently. Give your assistant ample time to share what difficulties your assistant is having with the relationship, too.

Seek guidance. If things do not improve after this initial conversation, seek guidance from a mentor or trusted adviser. Explain the specific problems that you are having and what steps you have taken to better the situation. Raise the option of a change of assistant and seek your mentor's counsel as to relevant firm policies, potential firm politics, and any other considerations.

Transition discreetly. If you decide to move forward with a change of administrative assistant, do so discreetly. Speak confidentially with whomever is in charge (this will likely be handled through the human resources (HR) department or a managing partner) and follow all firm policies. The news that you have changed your assistant should only be shared with the personnel in the office who need to know. If your colleagues ask, explain that you were simply seeking a "better fit" for your particular practice habits. Work closely with your new assistant to ensure a successful relationship from the beginning.

Paralegals

Working with a paralegal is not unlike working with an administrative assistant; however, there are typically fewer paralegals in any given firm, so you likely won't have a paralegal assigned to you. Rather, paralegals are staffed on projects the same way that attorneys are.

Paralegals have specialized training, and their work is fairly substantive. Their abilities and responsibilities vary widely from firm to firm. In some firms, paralegals perform legal research and draft certain basic documents. In others, they focus largely on document management. Of course, as with assistants, paralegals are not trained attorneys, so it is important to verify any work product done by a paralegal before it leaves your hands.

Your best bet is to befriend the paralegals in your department and learn from them. Let them teach you everything they know. This will be some of the best on-the-job training that you will receive.

Other Law Firm Staff

Law firms run on their staff members. The mail room, information technology department, law library, docket department, HR department, payroll department, and recruiting department, among many other departments, are made up of law firm staff members. Get to know as many staff members in the firm as you can. Get to know them by name. Think of them around the holidays. They are often the ones who need support and encouragement the most. And remember that a legal career is a demanding one. The more people you have rooting for you, supporting you, expediting your mail, pulling in obscure treatises via interlibrary loan, or whatever the case may be, the better your career will be for it.

11

WORKING WITH ATTORNEYS

In a law firm, you work "with" other attorneys, not "for" them. If you position yourself correctly, you will be just as significant as the most senior attorneys with whom you are working.

Positioning yourself correctly involves efficiently and effectively handling all aspects of the assignment process. You will have to understand how to solicit assignments, take assignments, complete assignments, present assignments, turn down assignments, approach your work holistically, and take credit for your work.

TIP
Never forgo the opportunity to make a positive impression.

Soliciting Assignments

As with any business proposition, you have to be proactive about getting staffed on projects and getting work. To play on the solo practitioner analogy from Chapter 4, filling your plate with work is key to your viability. The process of getting work, in and of itself, can say a lot about the kind of practitioner you are. It is, without a doubt, the perfect opportunity to make a positive impression.

As a new lawyer (or any lawyer looking for work), the best approach for soliciting work is to get up and walk around the office and introduce yourself. This indicates that you are engaged and genuinely care about the types of projects that you work on—as opposed to sending e-mails to solicit work, which potentially comes across as lacking effort and may be ignored. This also allows you to control some of the early impressions that you make on the attorneys in your firm and under what circumstances, too.

When you are making the rounds from office to office (or floor to floor, depending on how your firm is organized), be conscientious. Knock on each attorney's door even if the door is open. If someone is on the telephone, appears to be deep in thought, has people in the office or otherwise looks unavailable, come back another time. The last thing that you want to do is irritate or inconvenience someone before you've even introduced yourself.

Make the introduction very brief. Explain that you are new to the firm and want to introduce yourself. Be sure to indicate that you are looking for work and look forward to working with that attorney if and when the need arises.

If you are working in law firm with more than twenty senior (i.e., assigning) attorneys, consider staggering your introductions and solicitations for work (five a day is reasonable). This will help you manage your workload in the event that each introduction results in an assignment.

Finally, you want to make clear from the outset that you work well in teams. Your goal should be to work easily and comfortably with any team of attorneys and staff that is brought together. Be flexible, make accommodations, and modify your working style to benefit the group.

Taking Assignments

Let's assume that your introductions lead to assignments or that an assignment has come across your desk in some other way. The next step is understanding that there is a distinct art to taking an assignment. The following tips will help you hone that skill:

> **TIP**
> If you are meeting someone in your firm for the first time, an easy segue into a potential working relationship is simply to say, "Hi, [their first name]. I don't think we've met yet. I'm [your first name]."

Maintain a good attitude. Maintain a good attitude about any assignment you are given. Remember that every assignment presents a learning opportunity even if it does not feel substantive or significant at first glance.

Think quick (not quickly—though you should do that, too). In

TIP

Never go into another attorney's office without a pad of paper and pen in hand. You never know when an impromptu visit will materialize in an assignment, and you want to be in a position to take down an assignment whenever the opportunity presents itself.

other words, assume that the meeting will be a short one. For the most part, the assigning attorney is busy and is giving you an assignment so that the attorney is freed up to do something else. In a face-to-face or telephone meeting to get an assignment (as opposed to an e-mail assignment), while there is certainly no need to rush, you should be conscientious of the assigning attorney's time and not prolong the meeting unnecessarily.

Think opportunity. As with almost everything you will do in your early career, taking an assignment from a more senior attorney is an opportunity to make a good impression and build a relationship. Take advantage of the opportunity. Listen carefully to the assignment and take good notes as it is given. Do not interrupt. Ask thoughtful questions. At the end, reiterate the assignment in a short phrase or two to be sure that you are clear as to what you have been asked to do and to demonstrate to the assigning attorney that you are an engaged, responsible, reliable attorney.

Know your deadlines. Do not begin an assignment without a clear understanding of the deadline. If you are not told, ask at the time you are given the assignment, "When would you like me to get this to you?" Treat any deadline as a formal one. Calendar the deadline, and give yourself ample time to get the project done. If it is a rush project, get to it and get it done per the assigning attorney's expectations. If the assignment is taking longer than expected, approach the assigning attorney well in advance of the deadline and explain that you believe you can get a certain portion of the project done within the allotted time (be specific) but may require additional time to finalize the project.

TIP

If you must ask for an extension of time, do so well in advance of any deadline. Never wait until the day that an assignment is due to ask for an extension.

Know the form of delivery. You should not begin an assignment without a clear understanding of the form that the assignment will take. Be certain that you know, before you start working on the assignment, whether the assigning attorney expects a verbal report, a written document, a compilation of research, etc. This will guide the way that you approach the assignment and ensure that you are moving in the right direction from the outset.

Follow up thoughtfully. As you begin working on an assignment, you may find that you have follow-up questions. This is not only acceptable, it is a good opportunity to engage in intelligent, insightful conversation with the assigning attorney and keep the assigning attorney informed of the assignment status. Before you approach an assigning attorney with questions, however, be sure that the questions are thoughtful ones. Be sure that you have exhausted your resources. Do not ask questions to which you can easily find the answer elsewhere (e.g., by simply looking in a rule book).

TIP

When working on an assignment, do not assume that doing more than what was asked (e.g., a three-page memorandum instead of an e-mail memorandum or a memorandum in lengthy narrative paragraphs instead of bullet points) is necessarily better. Often, there are time constraints and billing constraints of which you are not aware that govern the type of work product asked of you.

Completing Assignments

Let's say that you have received an assignment from a partner, and you have encountered an issue that you need to discuss with the partner. You have called and e-mailed the partner. You have sent follow-up "friendly reminders." Still, you cannot get a response. This can be tricky, and it will require you to draw on all of the professional skills we have discussed at length.

As an initial step, you have to gauge the importance of the issue. Consider whether you actually need to speak with the assigning attorney. If you have simply written a memorandum and would like feedback, following up with the partner and reaching out repeatedly is not appropriate.

If, however, there is some urgency—if a document must be signed, if a client is waiting on your work product and you are waiting on the attorney before you can deliver it, or if there is a deadline—and you have not heard from the attorney despite several e-mail attempts, you are going to have to be proactive.

First, make every effort to see the partner in person; it is difficult to ignore someone who is standing right in front of you.

Second, let the partner's administrative assistant also know that you are looking for the partner. If you have a relationship with the assistant, ask if the assistant might be willing to send you an e-mail when the partner is in his office or to share the partner's cell phone number with you.

Third, connect with a mentor or a more senior associate who has worked with this partner before. You might discover that the partner tends to be slow at responding, and you may get some tips for how to elicit a response.

Finally, when all else fails and time pressures dictate, consider sending a self-executing e-mail with specific plans: "I plan on doing X, Y, and Z by this time if I don't hear otherwise from you." You may also want to document in the e-mail your diligence regarding the assignment: consider describing the efforts you have made to complete the assignment, including efforts to get advice or feedback from others in the assigning attorney's absence.

TIP

Rather than approaching an assigning attorney each time a question comes to mind, compile a number of questions that can be asked all at one time (preferably at a time that is convenient for the assigning attorney).

Presenting Assignments

Once an assignment is complete, think about the best way to deliver the assignment. If the assigning attorney asked for a verbal report of some kind (e.g., a follow-up conversation or meeting), stop by the attorney's office in person (do not send an e-mail unless, after several tries, you cannot locate the attorney) and indicate that you are available to speak about the assignment at any time that is convenient for the attorney. In advance of approaching the assigning attorney, prepare notes and key talking points. When you approach the assigning attorney, have all of the necessary materials with you (cases or statutes cited, other source material, etc.) and be prepared to discuss the assignment on the spot in the event that you are asked to do so.

If the assignment calls for written work product, deliver exactly what was asked. If you were asked to do an e-mail memorandum (i.e., a memorandum in the body of an e-mail instead of in a Word document as an attachment to the e-mail), submit an e-mail memorandum. Indicate in the e-mail that you are available to discuss the material or do any follow-up work as necessary. If you were asked to prepare a short, bullet-pointed memorandum, be sure to do exactly that. Whatever the case, you should listen carefully to your assignment and deliver on the assignment expectation.

For any written assignment, provide an

TIP

If the assigning attorney is not available, leave the assignment on the attorney's chair (not desk!) with a neatly written sticky note indicating what the assignment is, who it is from, and your direct extension. Leaving the assignment on the chair ensures that the assignment will not be overlooked.

electronic and a hard copy. E-mail the assignment first and indicate in the e-mail exactly what you are transmitting and that you will bring a hard copy to the assigning attorney following the e-mail. In the body of the e-mail, you should also briefly summarize the contents of the attachment in the event that the assigning attorney is viewing the e-mail on a handheld device and cannot see the attachment. If possible, after sending the e-mail, hand the hard copy to the assigning attorney in person.

As a final point, no matter what the assignment is, never turn in a draft or work in progress. You will always be expected to turn in your best, complete, final work product. If an assigning attorney says, "Get me a *draft* by Tuesday," that attorney is not asking for a rough draft. Rather, that attorney is saying, "Give me your best final work product by Tuesday."

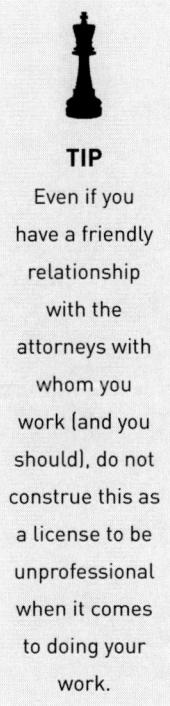

TIP

Even if you have a friendly relationship with the attorneys with whom you work (and you should), do not construe this as a license to be unprofessional when it comes to doing your work.

Turning Down Assignments

Whether a new lawyer may turn down an assignment at all is a point of contention. I believe that you can, but you have to earn the right to turn down work. And it is acceptable only where it is literally not feasible to accomplish the assignment. If there is any possible way to get the assignment done, you must.

If you are working Monday through Friday 9:00 a.m. to 5:00 p.m., you have a minimum workload and are not in a position to turn down work. If you are working Monday through Friday 8:00 a.m. to 6:00 p.m. or 7:00 p.m., you have a significant, though manageable, workload and are also not in a position to turn down work. If you are working six or seven days a week, eight to ten hours a day, you have a heavy workload and turning down work is appropriate.

There is a right way to turn down work. As we said earlier, anytime someone comes to you with a project, express interest and enthusiasm. If you are simply not in a position to do the work, explain that although you would like to assist, you have assignments pending from [name specific people] that have to be done by [state specific due dates].

If the new project is not an urgent one and can be completed after your more pressing projects are due, offer to take it on. If it is an urgent project and the assigning attorney needs your help despite your workload, the attorney will likely offer to approach the other attorneys with whom you are working and make arrangements.

In the rare instance that you are given the assignment anyway and left to figure out how to manage this on your own, do not panic. Go to your mentor and seek counsel. Consider

TIP

Your priority is to do good work. This is what people will remember. As a new lawyer, you may be tempted to take on every assignment offered to you; however, you should make sure that you never put yourself in a position where you are too overwhelmed to do your work well.

who the assigning attorneys are for each pending assignment. Go to the most approachable or most junior and explain your situation. If any of the deadlines are soft or negotiable, seek some additional time.

Workload aside, on certain occasions you may have a personal reason that a particular assignment deadline does not work for you. The personal reason has to be a very good one. Most personal events can be rescheduled. And, as a new lawyer, personal events should be scheduled carefully. If possible, schedule these events around key deadlines. Early in your career, schedule vacations sparingly and make them short. Once you have scheduled something, let the attorneys with whom you are working know well in advance and make sure that your workload is covered.

Approaching Your Work Overall

As you work on assignments, think holistically. Instead of completing one discreet project after another, become involved and invested in your cases as a whole. Follow up on work that you have done. Follow up on the status of the case or deal. Volunteer to take on additional work. This way, you are not only taking a holistic approach to your work, you are also building relationships.

TIP

If a scheduled vacation conflicts with an important project deadline, offer to cancel but do not actually do so unless you are expressly asked. More often than not, the assigning attorney will not want you to cancel and, with your help and forethought, will find another way to get the work done.

Taking Credit for Your Work

From time to time in a firm, someone may try to take credit for your work product. This happens typically in a situation where you, the junior associate, are working with a more senior associate and a partner. The senior associate directs you to do work; you turn it in to the senior associate; and the senior associate takes the work to the partner with few, if any, contributions of his own and takes credit for the work. This can be a difficult and frustrating situation.

However, this a situation that you can handle. As with all things in a firm, remember that this happens to everyone—you are not alone. Do not be personally offended. If anything, you should feel proud that your work is good enough that others want credit for it. It is important to remain reasonable. No confrontation or blowup is necessary or warranted. Rather, make a note to yourself of the work you have done on the case. Then, when the case is over or there is a slow period, approach the partner casually when the partner is not busy and say that you really enjoyed the work that you were assigned on the case. State specifically the work that you did and what you learned from it. Explain that you look forward to working with the partner going forward. That's all that you have to do.

12

SPEAKING LIKE A LAWYER

Language is the tool of lawyers. If used correctly, it is a powerful one.

Speaking with Colleagues in Informal Settings

In your early legal career, you will be interacting with your law firm colleagues quite a bit. Long before you are too busy on your own files to even look up from your desk, you are going to be: meeting people; taking assignments; and conversing about cases, projects, or deals.

I want you to see these conversations—everyday conversations with your colleagues—as opportunities. Welcome any conversation, both in passing and otherwise, with attorneys whom you know or whom you would like to get to know. Take the opportunity to demonstrate that you are an engaging, sociable person who has interesting things to say about legal and non-legal subjects. You also want to be sure that you are speaking with confidence; timidity and self-doubt are not well received in a law firm environment.

Speaking with Colleagues in Formal Settings

When speaking with your colleagues in more formal settings (e.g., internal meetings or conferences), the easiest way to be impressive is to prepare. Know your role in the meeting, and make an express plan for your participation. If you have been asked, for example, to deliver the results of some research or to recap the facts of a client's case or deal, prepare an organized outline with the key points that you want to make and any additional, relevant ideas. Anticipate questions and prepare answers. Have multiple copies on hand of any relevant materials.

TIP

When an attorney stops by your office casually and asks you how things are going, take advantage of this opportunity to demonstrate that you are an enthusiastic, constructive, productive member of your firm. Explain that you are enjoying your work. Follow this up with specifics. While being mindful of the attorney's time, add some depth and meaning to the interaction beyond the typical one-word answer, "Good."

Speaking with Clients

Your interactions with firm clients are the most important interactions that you will have, even if infrequent in the early years of your career. The firm runs on its clients. Making clients happy (e.g., by staffing projects with attorneys whom the clients know and like) is a priority.

In speaking with clients, your professionalism is going to be key. Your ability to be social will be of great value, too. Above all, you want to make clients feel that you are supremely competent and the best associate for the case, project, or deal.

TIP
This may be obvious, I admit, but: Do not chew gum in client meetings.

Speaking with Opposing Counsel

As a new lawyer, you might be surprised how quickly you will be required to speak with opposing counsel. Many things happen at the opposing counsel level. Agreements are made, deadlines are revised, and points of contention are resolved in routine conversations.

If asked to do so, you should feel comfortable and confident picking up the phone and calling your opposing counsel. While this is not always easy at first, it is something you will become accustomed to over time, and with practice. Early on, in order to overcome some

TIP
Never give away originals of any documents. In advance of any meeting, make photocopies and distribute the copies instead.

of the anxiety you may be feeling about the idea of calling opposing counsel, ask a mentor or more senior attorney if you may sit in on a call or two with an opposing counsel to gauge the proper approach. In speaking with opposing counsel, you should be professional and courteous. Civility is key. Set a respectful, cordial tone between the two of you.

Speaking a Foreign Language

This is somewhat of an aside but worth mentioning. From time to time in all law firms, but in large law firms in particular, a firmwide e-mail or other firm-wide request will go out seeking someone who speaks a foreign language. The e-mail may be seeking assistance in a client meeting or in the translation of documents or other written materials. Unless you are supremely proficient in a particular foreign language, be cautious about volunteering your help. It is very difficult to do legal work in a foreign language; it requires something significantly more demanding than the ability to speak conversationally in social situations. (By the way, I'm telling you this because, as a first year lawyer, I pulled an all-nighter on the phone with my mom, frantically seeking her assistance in translating complex business terms in Italian. I speak

TIP

Some opposing attorneys make a career out of being contentious. Do not let it get to you or inform the way that you practice. Do not respond in a similarly contentious manner. Model your practice after the kind of person you want to be— not the kind of person you dislike.

Italian fluently—along with English, it was my first language—but apparently I am not prepared to take on a high level Italian CEO who is embroiled in a messy breach of contract case.) As with all things, be clear at the outset about what help is being sought. Of course, volunteer your assistance if you are able.

13

WRITING LIKE A LAWYER

An attorney in my firm once told me there are no bad writers—only bad thinkers. At the time (I honestly think it was my first day at work), I was a little traumatized. On reflection, though, there is admittedly some value in this. Our writing skills are largely dependent on our ability to think clearly, organize, and edit with a critical eye—and that is something we, as lawyers, are trained to handle.

I read somewhere that the average lawyer writes more than the average novelist. Lawyers write a lot and are expected to be good at it.

Note Taking

As new lawyers, we tend to take note taking for granted. Early on, this will be one of your primary responsibilities. You will be expected to take copious, detailed notes and to be the keeper of those notes for any case, project, or deal that you are working on. In meetings, in particular, remember that the senior attorney is likely speaking or leading the meeting in some way and therefore is unable to take detailed notes. The attorney will count on you to essentially transcribe the meeting.

Before any meeting, prepare basic identifying notes: the name of the case or deal, the date, and the call-in telephone numbers, if relevant. In the meeting, note the names and job titles of everyone who participated and whether they participated over the phone or in person. And throughout the course of the meeting, make note of the complete substantive contents of the meeting unless instructed otherwise.

E-mail Writing

E-mail writing has supplanted nearly all other forms of communication, including everyday conversations. Because of our regular (incessant) use of e-mail, we have the tendency to think of it as an informal mode of communi-

TIP
Keep a designated pen and pad of paper next to your telephone. This way, you will be prepared to take down detailed notes of any phone call or message. If a phone message is important, forward it to your administrative assistant to transcribe, and convert the transcription into a memo to the file.

cation. In fact, in a law firm setting, it has taken the place of—and thus is equivalent to—other formal modes of communication.

E-mail writing style, like any legal writing style, is personal to some extent; and you will find your voice and improve your e-mail writing over time. However, there are some fundamental rules to live by as you begin drafting e-mails in a professional environment. Let's take a look at the discrete parts of a professional e-mail:

To. Direct an e-mail to anyone who is impacted by the e-mail or called upon to respond.

Carbon Copy (cc). Copy anyone who should be aware of the e-mail but who is not being addressed directly. When sending external e-mails (i.e., e-mails outside of the firm), you should typically copy the more senior attorneys with whom you are working.

Blind Carbon Copy (bcc). The blind copy allows you to include parties to an e-mail that you would like to be aware of the communication without others knowing. Use this sparingly. Consider whether your objectives can be met by forwarding the

TIP

As the junior associate, you will be expected to know the number of anyone you may have to call during a meeting (client, co-counsel, opposing counsel, judge's clerk, etc.). Have those numbers on hand in the event that you are asked for them.

TIP

Verify the spelling of all addressees' first and last names.

TIP

Verify all e-mail addresses before sending an e-mail. In addition, turn off the AutoFill feature in your e-mail program.

e-mail after it has been sent instead.

Subject Line. The subject line of any e-mail should be a substantive, meaningful one. The recipient should know by looking at the e-mail exactly what subject it covers. For example, include the relevant case caption or deal and a short synopsis of specific topics covered in the e-mail. Generally, the more detail, the better.

Salutation. In e-mail writing, it is customary to omit the words *Dear* or *Hi*. Simply begin the e-mail with the addressee's name. For external e-mails, use *Mr.* or *Ms.* in your first communication with someone, and continue to refer to that person by title until otherwise instructed (e.g., when the person signs a response e-mail by first name or you meet in person and are instructed to use a first name). Likewise, do not abbreviate first names (e.g., *Michael* to *Mike*) unless expressly instructed.

Key E-mail Phrases. As with all legal writing, in e-mail writing you want to take care to orient the reader.

Some standard introductory e-mail phrases include the following:

- I write concerning . . .
- I write in regard to . . .
- I write to remind you . . .
- I write pursuant to Rule ____ of the ____ Rules.

- The purpose of this e-mail is to [remind, confirm, transmit] . . .
- Per your request, . . .

Some key phrases to rely on as you are concluding an e-mail include the following:

- Please let me know if you would like me to [follow up, continue, look into this further]. . .
- I look forward to hearing from you at your convenience.
- Please let me know at your earliest convenience.
- Please do not hesitate to contact me if . . .

TIP

When e-mailing a client, consider whether a "Privileged and Confidential—Attorney-Client Communication—Attorney Work Product—Do Not Forward" tag in the subject line is appropriate.

Attachments. You will routinely attach documents to e-mails. Choose a reliable orienting phrase for attaching documents, and use this phrase again and again.

And be sure to actually attach the document! Here is my foolproof way to ensure that you do not send an e-mail that references an attachment without

TIP

When attaching a completed, final document, use the phrase "Attached please find. . . ." For any draft, use the phrase "Attached for your review and comment please find. . . ."

actually attaching the document (which requires an embarrassing follow-up apology e-mail):

The moment you type the word *attached*, STOP! Literally, do not write another word. Attach the document to the e-mail. Open the attachment to be sure it is the correct one. Then continue writing.

Signature Block. Craft an automatic signature block that appears at the end of all of your e-mails. Use a firm template or copy a template from a senior attorney in your firm.

Substance. No matter how long or short, your e-mails should be well thought out, well organized, and well written. Use topic sentences. Use transitional words and phrases.

For lengthier e-mails or e-mails that address multiple, related topics, include headings and subheadings.

Proofread your e-mails meticulously. Read them aloud before sending. For a longer or more substantive e-mail, print the e-mail and read it in hard copy before sending.

And, where possible, avoid writing lengthy, substantive e-mails from your handheld device. You are bound to make mistakes or to omit substance due to the inherent limitations of writing on a handheld device. (For a sample e-mail, please see Appendix 1.)

TIP
Do not use contractions, emoticons, or informal language in professional e-mails.

TIP
Remove the automatic "Sent from my handheld device" insignia from your e-mails. It needlessly lets people know that you are out of the office.

Responding to E-mails

As a lawyer and a professional, you will be expected to respond in a timely, thorough manner to every e-mail that you receive. This is one of the most important aspects of e-mail writing.

Respond promptly to internal e-mails (i.e., e-mails sent from colleagues in your firm) and any e-mails from clients. In no instance should you let more than three hours go by, within reason: if you get an e-mail at 3:00 a.m., in a reasonable world and barring exceptional circumstances—for example, if you are working with foreign clients and knew that the e-mail was coming—you can respond during regular office hours.

If you are delayed more than three hours, open your response e-mail with an apology for the delay. If you have a good reason, state that, too (e.g., you were out of the office on another matter).

For external e-mails, you should respond within the same day if possible. And certainly respond within twenty-four hours without exception.

TIP

Respond fully to any e-mail that you receive. If you are asked about three items or asked to complete three tasks, address all three in your response e-mail. Do not leave anything open-ended. Do not leave the recipient wondering if you have done all of what was asked of you.

Miscellaneous E-mail Advice

E-mail writing etiquette is a continually evolving subject. Here is some quick advice on various e-mail-related topics:

- Use "Reply All" sparingly, if at all.
- Do not mindlessly forward e-mails: review the entire chain to be sure that an e-mail should be forwarded, and be sensitive to whether the person who sent you the e-mail would like for you to forward it. You may consider starting a new thread and recapping the email instead.
- Be very careful with your contacts: you do not want to send a privileged e-mail to a nonprivileged party with a similar name.
- Avoid personal e-mail correspondence and junk e-mail at work.
- Recalling e-mails rarely, if ever, works, so don't try to recall a message unless you are absolutely desperate (and have a plan B. in place, too!).

TIP

Anytime you are going to be away from your desk for more than a day, set up an automated out-of-office reply thanking the sender for the e-mail, indicating that you are out of the office, stating how long you will be out, and specifying whom to contact in your absence.

Letter Writing

Letter writing is a lot like e-mail writing: it will likely comprise a large portion of the work that you will do in your career, and your writing must adhere to certain professional standards. Since we went over e-mails in detail, I'll share just a few additional points that are unique to letters:

Above the Fold. Letters will typically contain your firm letterhead and contact information at the top. If your contact information is automatically populated, be sure that it is entered correctly the first time.

Likewise, your letter will contain the addressee's contact information above the fold. Verify that this information is also correct.

It is also customary to indicate above the fold the means of transmittal of the letter (e.g., fax, USPS, FedEx, messenger, etc.). Whether you send a letter overnight, via Saturday delivery, etc., will depend on urgency, expectations of the recipient, course of dealings, and any legal or statutory considerations.

Subject Line. As with e-mails, the subject line of a letter should be a meaningful one. It should be informative, too. Include the case or deal caption. Include a short synopsis of the letter subject. In addition, consider any client-specific tag lines.

Salutation. In a letter, unlike in an e-mail, you want to use *Dear*. As with an e-mail, use *Mr.* or *Ms.* until otherwise notified.

Closing. Use a formal closing when signing off on a letter. Yours truly, Best regards, Sincerely, Warmly, or a similar firm default closing is proper.

TIP

As a related matter, you will be expected to return telephone calls in a timely manner. For internal calls, respond immediately. For client calls, if applicable, prepare first and then return the call. In no event should more than twenty-four hours go by before you respond to a client.

TIP

Do not use firm letterhead for personal letter correspondence.

TIP

Write *Esq.* after the name of any attorney copied on a letter. This makes identifying privileged letters, if and when the time comes, easier.

Enclosures. In your letter, note whether there are any enclosures (typically, use the phrases "Enclosed please find . . ." or "I have enclosed for your review . . ."), and be sure to actually enclose.

Carbon Copy (cc). In a letter, the "cc" is usually placed at the end. Typically, you will cc the senior attorneys with whom you are working.

Blind Copy (bcc). In a letter, each "bcc" recipient is set forth on a separate page. The bcc page is sent to the bcc recipient only, and each bcc recipient should not know who else received the letter via bcc.

Substance. A letter adheres to all basic legal writing principles. It should be formal and well organized. Use headings and topic sentences to guide the reader.

Certain statements work well in certain situations. If your letter is the first correspondence between parties, begin with a statement identifying whom you represent (typically, *Please be advised that we represent . . .*). If you are initiating correspondence (where prior correspondence has occurred), *I write concerning . . .* or *The purpose of this letter is to . . .* is proper. If responding to a letter, *I am in receipt of your letter dated X* is a good way to begin. If a letter is for settlement purposes, you should add the disclaimer, *This letter is for settlement purposes only*. This is important because it will ensure that under the Federal Rules or any corresponding state rules, the letter is regarded as an inadmissible offer of compromise. In other words, if the case does not settle, the contents of the letter will be inadmissible to prove your client's liability later on. Finally, letters are also excellent tools for reiterating agreements: *As agreed during our telephone conversation on X date . . .* is one way to begin such a letter. (For a sample letter, please see Appendix 2.)

Billing Time

Depending on the type of legal work you are doing, billing time may be a significant part of your daily written practice. Defense attorneys bill their time almost without exception. Plaintiffs' firms typically do not bill time (but do often catalog costs and other expenses).

Methods of Billing Time

Whether it is a significant part of your daily practice or not, it is a good idea to have some background in how to do it correctly. There are a number of ways to bill time.

Hourly billing is a way of recording how much time you have

TIP

Learn when your law firm mailroom closes, and keep this information posted in your office at all times. Know the location of the nearest FedEx or other late-night mail services in case you need to ship something on your own after hours.

spent on work for a specific client on a specific day. In a firm that bills clients by the hour, each attorney has a billable rate. For example, as a new lawyer, your billable rate may be $160 per hour. If you spend an hour on a project for a client, that client will owe the firm $160 for your work.

Fixed flat fee billing is used in certain practice areas more than others and is becoming more popular in big law firms. In a fixed fee scenario, the firm negotiates a price with the client in advance. This price may be task related or case related. For example, a client may agree to pay $1 million for an entire year's worth of work. Or a client may agree to pay a $30,000 flat fee for a summary judgment brief. The trick for the firm in these situations is to keep the billable time below the flat rate; otherwise, it is not a financially beneficial arrangement for the firm. For clients, the assurance of paying a set amount instead of receiving a surprise bill in an unexpected amount is a strong incentive to negotiate a flat fee arrangement.

Contingent fees are more straightforward. These are often implemented in plaintiff-oriented litigation firms. In cases that are handled on a contingent fee basis, the firm

TIP

Copy letters and any enclosures before mailing. A letter should not leave your office until a copy is filed away in a correspondence rack.

TIP

It is customary to bill by the tenth of the hour: one hour of billable time equals six minutes of work.

gets no money up front but recovers a percentage (typically one-third) of any award that the plaintiff receives (whether the case settles or goes to trial). This could also apply to transactional work, but it is more commonly seen in litigation.

Billing Time: More Than Money

Billing time presents its own unique set of opportunities. Although it may seem insignificant and although it is in some ways routine, your bills will say a lot about the type of practitioner you are.

Remember that the attorney you work with on any billable matter will be reviewing your bills in detail. On top of that, the client will be reviewing the bills in detail. Your objective, as always, is to impress both the attorneys with whom you are working and the firm clients.

Treat each entry on your time sheet as a mini-memorandum. Create a progression, or story, from one day to the next. Include enough detail so that the client can quantify the work you have done, but not so much detail

TIP

Do not leave for the day unless your time sheets are done. This will ensure accurate billing and will protect you from losing billable time.

TIP

Your time sheets will go before the client with your name directly next to each entry. This is your introduction to the client and an easy opportunity to be impressive.

TIP

Every attorney and client has particularities and nuances in how they expect time entries to look. When you begin working on a client matter, review prior bills submitted to the client by the attorney with whom you are working. This will give you insight into how both the attorney and the client prefer their bills.

that it is overwhelming or unhelpful. Do not bill for mundane or administrative tasks that you should not be doing (e.g., photocopying documents or sealing envelopes—can you imagine paying a lawyer to do that?). Be consistent in your references: do not write *J. Doe*, *John Doe*, etc., to refer to the same person in the same bill. And be conscientious about how you refer to your client: use the client's name and not simply *Client* when referring to your client in bills.

As a new lawyer, you may feel that your substantive work or exposure to clients is limited. This is not actually the case. Your billable time entries constitute substantive work product that goes directly before the client every month. In other words, the client will see your work product from your first day at the firm and thereafter. This is a great opportunity to show the client that you are an intelligent, thoughtful, impressive practitioner. (For a sample time entry, please see Appendix 3.)

14

FEEDBACK

I have seen many new lawyers struggle with the concept of feedback in a law firm. There is this (not unreasonable) expectation that as part of working in a collaborative, professional environment, feedback will be given readily and work product will be reviewed, revised, and further improved upon based on this feedback. In reality, the feedback that you will receive on any given assignment will vary greatly from assignment to assignment and attorney to attorney depending on time pressures, personality traits, and the workload of the attorneys involved.

No Feedback

It is not entirely uncommon to receive no feedback on an assignment. In fact, this happens fairly regularly. You should not construe this, necessarily, as a sign that you did not do a good job. Oftentimes, the attorney has forgotten about the work product or is simply too busy to get back to you. In this instance, if you are concerned, check in with your mentor as to whether the assigning attorney typically gives feedback (your mentor may also know whether the attorney is busy on another matter). Alternatively, after some time has passed, consider stopping by or sending a quick e-mail to the attorney offering to follow up on the work that you did. This will frequently result in follow-up work or some affirmation of the work that you did previously.

A Lot of Feedback

At the opposite end of the spectrum, on occasion an attorney may return work to you with so much red ink that your inclination is to have a heart attack on the spot (or maybe the attorney had a heart attack, and that's why there is so much red). Again, this does not necessarily mean that you have done something wrong. Many attorneys are particular when it comes to writing, and they are inclined to edit or rewrite anything that is given to them.

The best way to handle this situation is to genuinely learn from the comments. Study the preferences and nuances of the assigning attorney so that you can accommodate the attorney (and save some of the red ink) on the next project. No matter what, learn—do not make value judgments (i.e., the assigning attorney is just a bad writer or does not understand your writing style). Finally, do not be discouraged. This happens to everyone. It is just part of the learning process.

Now, with this said, if you have done a poor job and this is reflected in the comments, it will be your responsibility to approach the assigning attorney, express appreciation for the feedback, and explain that you have made notes about the various ways that your work product could have been better. Let the attorney know that, going forward, it will be decidedly better. Then, go about improving your work product with sincere dedication and effort.

Yearly Reviews

Typically, yearly reviews are conducted by a partner or partners in your department or office. Occasionally, if you work in a national law firm, for example, your review may be run by a managing partner or partners from the firm's headquarters. The attorneys with whom you have worked throughout the year will fill out detailed evaluations of your performance in advance of the review, and the designated reviewing partners will summarize or recap those reviews and go through them with you. Expect that they will highlight your strengths and weaknesses as well as goals to work toward in the upcoming year.

As with any meeting in a law firm, go in prepared. In the case of your reviews, you want to go in exceedingly prepared with notes, questions, and any other aspects of your career that you would like to discuss.

Take positive comments in a humble manner. Learn from the positive comments what is resonating with the attorneys in your firm and be sure to continue to build on this going forward.

TIP

If you receive a negative review that is unanticipated or that you feel is unwarranted, make clear that you were not aware of the situation but that you are thankful for hearing of it and will be sure that it does not happen again. Remember that your demeanor in your review can be as important as any of your work that is being reviewed.

If you receive a negative review, do not act defensively or get upset. Listen, accept the negative criticism, and ask for suggestions about how to avoid the same situation from occurring in the future. If you have already taken action, for example, if you have made a mistake and have worked to correct the mistake, explain clearly and succinctly in your review what measures you have taken and what you have learned from the experience. If you have had a particularly negative experience with a more senior attorney and anticipate a negative review, be prepared to explain what happened, but do not make excuses or speak negatively about the more senior attorney.

As a final point, be sure to share your goals for the upcoming year in your review and ask for feedback as to how you can ensure that you accomplish your goals. This will also demonstrate to your reviewers that you are proactively thinking about your career and development as an attorney.

TIP

Once you have been at the firm for a year or more, you should bring your goals from the previous year into the review with you. Remind the reviewers of the goals you had set for the prior year and that you accomplished those goals.

15

MISTAKES

It was late in the afternoon. I ran over to the after-hours assistant's desk and handed her a binder. The binder contained significant work product, correspondence with the client, and other key documents in our case. I asked her to photocopy the flagged documents in the binder and fax them over to my opposing counsel right away. The documents were due to him that day, or he would bring a motion before the court.

Nearly forty minutes later, just as I was starting to wonder, the assistant returned to my office. As she handed me the binder, she explained that it took her longer than expected to fax each and every document in the binder but that she managed it. Every document? Please let me have misunderstood. But no—I heard her correctly. Instead of faxing the few, carefully selected flagged documents, she had sent everything in the binder: work product, client confidences, and case strategy. I literally died on the spot. This was the biggest error of my career.

Thank the law firm gods for Mike, the assigning attorney on the case, a former assistant attorney general and seasoned law firm partner who had seen everything in his career and thought precisely nothing was a big deal. He talked me down from the ledge, and we worked together to get the documents back. In the end, even something of that magnitude ended up being all right.

When I explained to the assistant what had happened, she ran frantically from my office exclaiming, "It's not my fault!," with her wild curly black hair flailing behind her. Hysterical, in retrospect. It was definitely not her fault, though. It was mine. And if you are confused as to why, go back and read the earlier section on working with administrative assistants.

Practicing law is nuanced and, particularly in the beginning, comes with a steep learning curve. Because of this, on occasion, every lawyer makes mistakes. It's not only a fact, it is expected from lawyers early in their careers. What will set you apart, however, is your strategy for dealing with mistakes and how you move forward in the aftermath.

Let's assume that you have made a mistake. Here are some simple coping guidelines:

Don't panic. Although it will not feel like it in the moment, the majority of mistakes that you will make as a new lawyer are not fatal and can be fixed. If you panic, you will not be in the proper frame of mind to deal with the mistake. No matter what, never try to cover up the mistake.

Speak with your mentor. Find your mentor or someone you trust immediately. Work quickly with your mentor to figure out exactly what went wrong and why and to devise a strategy for approaching the attorney with whom you are working. Your mentor should help you devise a clear proposal for a solution.

This step is critical. The mistake likely stemmed from some lack of skill on your part; if you do not rely on a more senior or experienced attorney, you will not have the tools to make the situation better.

Approach the attorney with whom you are working. Before you attempt to fix the mistake based on the plan that you have devised with your mentor, you must approach the attorney with whom you are working. You want to get clearance from that attorney regarding how to move forward.

TIP

When you approach an assigning attorney about a mistake that you have made, consider this simple script: "I inadvertently [describe the mistake]. I am truly sorry. If you agree, I will [describe course of action for fixing the mistake]."

In approaching the attorney, explain in a straightforward manner that you have made a mistake. Do not make excuses. Do not blame anyone. Be direct and concise. Propose a clear plan for fixing the mistake.

TIP

Apologize genuinely and sincerely for any mistake that you make, but apologize only once. A repeated apology detracts from the sincerity and will only serve to negatively define your relationship with the attorney.

In the aftermath, work hard to fix the mistake. Do not make the same mistake again (ever!). If you work in a law firm that bills hours, offer to fix the mistake without billing your time for doing so. It is also a good idea going forward to go out of your way for the attorney in order to repair any negative impression that you may have made.

Recognize that life goes on. Do not dwell on your mistake, talk excessively about it with colleagues who otherwise do not need to know, or let it define your career. It's a long career, after all, and no single victory or defeat will say everything about the lawyer you are.

16

MARKETING

I sat across from an attorney in a mediation who told me two things that I'll never forget: (1) his son is a better-looking version of Brad Pitt (ummm . . .?); and (2) he fired an associate on the spot when the associate expressed that he had reservations about asking his friends and family for business. If you don't have the guts to ask your friends and family for business, this lawyer explained, you are never going to ask anyone for business, ever.

He was clearly a little unusual, but he did have a small point. The most successful lawyers are businesspeople. Period. As your career advances, there is little value in being the best issue spotter or a walking hornbook. Rather, you have to be a salesperson, and you have to know how to get business.

This is not something that you will ever learn in law school or in your law firm. In fact, if you are typical, you will spend eight to ten years practicing before you realize that you are going to have to bring in business of your own. And at that point, it is difficult to do so.

Lawyers, particularly those who bill time, are accustomed to a one-for-one proposition of work and reward. Work one hour, bill one hour. Work for a pay period, collect a paycheck. It's all measurable. Business development, on the other hand, is not. It takes years to build relationships that are significant enough to materialize in business. Even when the relationship is there, it may take years for the person with whom you are connected to be in a position to give you business. You have to be patient, and you have to put a lot of effort in knowing that it may be a very long time before you reap any benefits. This is why starting early in your career with business development is smart, even if not instantly rewarding.

Internal Marketing

In your early career, the bulk of your work will come internally from senior associates and partners. Therefore, you want to market yourself—and your practice—within your firm as a first step. The following are ways to accomplish this:

Do good work. The best way to get work from your colleagues is to do good work every time. Work hard. Learn your practice area. Consistently put out good work product. If your colleagues know that they can rely on you to do good work, you will never be short on assignments or billable hours. And in turn, you will have exposure to high-level work and interactions with clients sooner. This is a great first step in building your own book of work.

Participate in nonbillable work. Participate in nonbillable or non-business-generating firm events as often as possible. Join the recruiting committee, assist with an internal firm publication, act as a mentor, participate in pro bono work, prepare client pitches—these efforts will make you stand out as a superstar associate and will secure your position in the firm.

Know your firm. Earlier, we talked about how law firms are structured and how your success in the firm will depend on your understanding of this. Take some time early in your practice to learn not only how your firm is structured but also about the specific internal workings of your law firm. You should know every city where your law firm has an office. You should know the first and last names of the managing partners of every office and every department. Know the top partners in any practice area in which you are interested. Know what your firm specializes in and whether your firm is working on any particularly big (or newsworthy) deals or cases.

Learn your firm policies, too. Among many other things, your

TIP
When you begin practicing, you will likely receive a packet of materials, including your firm policies. Take these home and read them. Highlight any important provisions. Keep them readily available in the event that you need to reference them.

firm policies will tell you the following: whether you can expense cab receipts or dinner and under what circumstances; your health-care benefits; restrictions on buying and selling stock; how many vacation and sick days you have; how much time off you may take; whether you may teach classes at a local law school; and the firm's hiring and firing policies.

Keep up with legal news and current events. The most successful attorneys I know make a point of keeping up with legal news and other current events. Whether they follow recent Supreme Court decisions, the *ABA Journal*, weekly publications from city and state bar associations, the *National Law Review*, the *Wall Street Journal*, or other news sources, reading about legal and current events is integral to their daily routine.

As a new lawyer, the importance of keeping up with legal news cannot be overstated. By doing this, you will be able to contribute meaningfully to conversations with your law firm colleagues about cutting-edge legal information, you will be one of the first to learn of developments in the law that may impact your firm or your firm's clients, and you will be building a foundation for locating and

TIP

Twitter is an excellent resource for keeping up with legal news. All of the leading legal publications are on Twitter, and these publications post news and other information regularly. If you follow these sources on Twitter, all of your legal news will be compiled in one place, and you can comb through your Twitter feed for articles of interest.

connecting with potential clients. In order to keep up with legal news efficiently, you should devise a strategy that works for you (reading each and every publication daily is not realistic, of course).

Keeping up with legal and other news is a great internal marketing strategy in a more direct way, too. If you come across an article or information that may be of interest to a colleague in your office, even if that colleague is in an office overseas and you have never met before, an easy way to make an introduction and get to know them is to send along the article or information with a quick introduction of yourself and your practice (this is one way in which knowing your firm will come in handy). This will show that you are forward thinking and a relationship builder, and you will be top of mind when that attorney needs assistance from an associate in your office.

TIP

Have your business cards on you at all times. Put business cards in every suit coat, jacket pocket, purse, clutch, and wallet that you have. Put business cards in between your handheld device and the case it is in, too. This way, you will have cards on you when you are participating in meetings internally in your firm as well as when you are out and about.

External Marketing

You should also spend a bit of time each week on more traditional marketing outside of the office. The following are ways to accomplish this:

Establish contacts. Building your book of contacts is an easy and effective marketing tool. Anytime you meet anyone, whether it is an opposing counsel, an expert witness, a co-counsel, a court reporter, or a low-level employee at a corporation, collect their business card and input that person's information into your contacts with some detailed reminders about who that person is. Find reasons to reach out to your contacts from time to time. Consider sending them an article or an invitation to a free event. You never know when a contact will materialize in a true relationship or when someone is going to be able to help you in your career.

Join bar associations. Becoming involved in your local and state bar associations is a great way to network. Bar associations often put on social and educational events for members as well as provide opportunities to join specific divisions, journals, clubs, or committees.

Attend law school alumni networking events. Stay in touch with your law school friends. Many of your law school friends will be potential clients when they go in-house in the future.

Stay in touch with your friends. As a new lawyer, your busy practice is going to take priority over almost everything else, including your friendships with people outside of work. Make some effort to stay in touch with your friends outside of the law. These may prove to be your most important connections, and it is good for your well-being too (more on that soon).

Consider cross-marketing. As a new lawyer, you may not be able to offer substantive services at the outset. However, you should listen closely to the legal needs of the people around you. Can you refer someone to the more senior attorneys in your firm? Can you refer someone to an attorney outside of your firm who specializes in an area that your firm does not? Any referrals that you give will materialize in referrals for you later on.

Publish articles in law journals and other publications. As your career progresses, and if your firm policies permit, publishing articles in law journals and other legal publications is a great way to market your services. By virtue of associating your name with a published work, you are likely to be elevated to "expert" or "authority" status on a particular topic. And, over time, if you are publishing regularly enough, you will be designated "the" expert or authority on a particular topic. There is no better marketing angle than this.

Participate in continuing legal education (CLE) programs. Lawyers in most states are required to participate in a certain number of CLE programs every year. CLE programs are offered by local and state bar associations, various private companies, and most law firms.

There are two ways to approach obtaining CLE credits. As one option, you can attend the programs with your handheld device in hand, get work done while you are there, learn nothing, meet no one, collect your credit hours, and move on with your life—this approach is not recommended. The other option—the recommended one—is to approach CLE programs as marketing opportunities as well as opportunities to better your practice. CLE programs offered outside of your law firm, in particular, present easy opportunities to meet colleagues in your legal community. Attending CLE programs that attract in-house attorneys is a great way to get to know potential clients and establish other connections that you may not otherwise have occasion to foster. Making introductions, exchanging business cards, and demonstrating a genuine interest in what other attendees do are good first steps to networking effectively at these events.

As you gain more experience in your practice, arrange to present regularly at CLE programs. Much like publishing articles, this is a great way to establish yourself as an expert in a particular field. If you are wondering how you might go about presenting at a CLE program, consider simply asking. You would be surprised how often bar associations in particular are in need of presenters and will happily take volunteers.

Finally, as long as you are in attendance at CLE programs, you may as well be open to learning. This alone will put you ahead of just about everyone else in the room.

Don't neglect the intangibles. Treat your professional life as an interview. Any conversation, interaction, or observation can potentially lead to a career advancement for you. Think about this in your daily interactions with colleagues, clients, and friends.

TIP

Never publicly complain about your current job. This reflects badly on you. Also, if you are complaining or criticizing your current employer, others likely will not want to hire you. They won't send you business, either, because they have learned from you that your firm is not a good one.

17

SOCIAL MEDIA AND YOUR LEGAL PRACTICE

Joe (not his real name) walked by the big glass conference rooms on the thirty-first floor one afternoon. He saw that several of his colleagues were in a meeting with a high-profile professional athlete. He went back to his desk, logged onto Facebook, and told all 556 of his closest friends what he saw. He was fired the next day. For some context (though it's not required—the conduct was inappropriate no matter the context), this athlete was involved in a highly sensitive, private legal matter and wanted no one—especially the press—to know about it. This was an inexcusable screwup.

We are increasingly accustomed to sharing every aspect of our lives through social media. Contemporary social media sites have provided us with easy platforms for divulging information without any boundaries. What's more, we've come to believe that this is a natural way of behaving.

Now that you are a lawyer (and a professional), your approach to social media should be tailored accordingly. Using social media improperly can be detrimental to a legal career. On the other hand, using social media as a tool for enhancing your legal practice will set you apart from your peers and will make you an invaluable member of any legal team.

Using Social Media as a Professional

As a professional and an officer of the court, there are certain social media rules to live by.

Your social media profiles and any accompanying pictures should be set to private. Anything that others can

TIP

While we are on the topic of behaving professionally and ethically, do not give friends and family legal advice without clearing conflicts. This is potentially unethical and could create significant problems for your firm. As an example, your mother asks you to write a scathing letter on her behalf to an insurance company. You do so—and learn afterward that the insurance company is a longtime client of your firm. You—and, by extension, your firm—have now violated the ethical rules by simultaneously representing opposing parties.

view should reflect that you are a responsible, professional person.

Your professional life has no business making any appearances on social media, whether you are commenting, sharing, explaining, or otherwise, except for purposes of furthering your development as an attorney (e.g., through strategic use of LinkedIn, a business-oriented social networking site discussed in some detail below). Never share anything about your work or your clients with anyone outside of your practice, and especially not on any social media sites. If you do so, you are not only acting unprofessionally, you may be violating your ethical responsibility to maintain client confidences. If you would like to speak with family and friends about the work you are doing, describe your work in general terms but err on the side of caution and do not use client names.

You should not, under any circumstances, speak badly about your firm, your colleagues, or your work on social media sites, either. Again, not only is this unprofessional, but it will also create a problematic "paper" trail for you in the event that your job is ever on the line. Instead, speak privately with someone whom you trust outside of the firm about any frustrations that you may be having.

There are so many real implications to using social media improperly with respect to your practice, and it is simply not worth tempting fate.

Using Social Media to Enhance Your Legal Practice

Despite the professional responsibility implications of using social media, there are a number of significant possibilities for using social media to enhance your practice. Although the precise social media tools are constantly changing, the principles will undoubt-

TIP

Google yourself periodically and review the results. You want to be sure that if your clients, colleagues, or opposing counsel do background research on you, the results are positive.

edly be timeless. Currently, there are a number of sites that have set the framework for contemporary social media as we know it:

Facebook. Facebook is a social networking tool that allows you, the user, to connect with people whom you know. Through Facebook, you have wide latitude to reach out to people with whom you have been acquainted in your lifetime, even if only superficially. As we just discussed, as a lawyer, whether you work in a small or large law firm or government entity or otherwise, it is important to stay connected with potential clients and referral sources. Facebook offers an easy way to do this.

LinkedIn. LinkedIn is a business-oriented social networking site. LinkedIn allows you to connect with friends, classmates, and colleagues. Your LinkedIn profile will typically identify your employer and other business-related information about you. LinkedIn also supports business-oriented groups that you may be interested in joining. The advantages of joining LinkedIn include staying in touch with colleagues and potential clients, joining groups that are relevant to your legal practice so that you are kept apprised of developments in the law in your practice area and become familiar with others who share the same legal interests, and building your professional persona beyond the four corners of your office.

YouTube. YouTube is a video-hosting website where users can upload, share, and view videos. There is a YouTube video for virtually every subject matter imaginable. YouTube is not often the first thought when contemplating social media for lawyers. And it is rarely considered in a professional development context.

However, I have a suggestion for using YouTube to enhance your practice that I know will serve you well. In a legal context, YouTube is an excellent resource for self-education. Often, you will find yourself in the throes of a case or deal without a great understanding of what exactly your client does. This lack of understanding can be a barrier to your ability to assist on the case or deal. Through YouTube, you can watch and learn about your client's business, whether your client offers a service, product, or otherwise. As an example, if your client manufactures pressure washers and you are working on a case that deals with precisely how these pressure washers are manufactured, YouTube is an excellent resource for learning this. If you are working on a deal between two banks, YouTube has many excellent videos concerning secured transactions, the current debt crisis, and anything else you can think of that might be relevant to the banking industry. If you are lost in the subject matter of a case or deal, turn to YouTube for help.

Twitter. Twitter is my personal favorite of the existing social media sites. Twitter presents so many opportunities to grow your legal practice.

Twitter facilitates keeping up with legal, nonlegal, and client-related news and, as mentioned earlier, provides an easy, efficient way to do so. With Twitter, you can follow all of your favorite news sources (the *New York Times*, the *Wall Street Journal*, the *National Law Journal*, the American Bar Association, etc., are on Twitter), as well as many potential and actual clients (most corporations, large and small, are on Twitter). While you sip your morning coffee or on your commute to work (but probably not while driving!), scroll through your Twitter feed for headlines of interest. By 9:00 a.m., you will have caught up with the important news of the day and will be equipped to discuss this news with (i.e., impress) fellow associates, partners, or clients, as the case may be.

Twitter also supports conversation. Unlike other social media sites, with Twitter you have the ability to connect with other users whether they follow you or not. In other words, you can direct a tweet (a 140-character message) to anyone who is on Twitter. This means that you can speak with people whom you would otherwise have no way of contacting. You will be surprised how often someone will write back and how this can be the start of a lucrative relationship.

Twitter also builds communities. As you build relationships with other Twitter users, you will find that those users are connected with even more users who may be of interest to you. Suddenly, you find yourself in routine contact or conversation not only with people you have contacted but also with other users who share common interests. A Twitter community can provide resources, information, and support as you navigate your practice.

TIP

Check out your Facebook "friends," and find out where they work. You want to stay in regular touch with friends who may prove to be potential clients in the future. From time to time, reach out to those friends with an article or event that may be of interest to them.

18

HEALTH AND WELLNESS

In the early years of your practice, it is tempting to focus exclusively on work and compromise fundamental aspects of life outside of work, including basic health and wellness. Although hard work and dedication are admirable—and, indeed, required of legal professionals—maintaining good health is essential, too. Without it, being a top practitioner, or even meeting minimum expectations in your practice, will be difficult if not impossible.

In preparing this section (and in designing my programs for new lawyers), I thought a lot about what worked for me in my practice. I also interviewed many attorneys about their own health and wellness practices. At bottom, maintaining a work-life balance and savoring time outside of work are instrumental in preserving health and wellness.

For more specific advice, I consulted with Brooke, a friend and colleague who left her Big Law practice to become a therapist. Brooke enlightened me on the topic of self-care, something that is widely practiced by mental health professionals but rarely by attorneys. In short, self-care is a means for ensuring that while you are expending energy on the people, relationships, and work all around you, you are also making time to take care of yourself. By implementing self-care in your daily routine, you will ultimately be better positioned to do your job and better able to provide for clients, colleagues, and superiors.

To get you started, together with the help of our lawyer colleagues, Brooke and I built a self-care inventory that you can use in your daily practice to ensure that you are taking care of your own physical and mental well-being first and foremost.

Self-Care Inventory for Lawyers

Try to incorporate items from each category into your life on a regular basis.

Physical Self-Care

_____ Eat healthful foods, including breakfast, daily.
_____ Get exercise.
_____ Get sleep.
_____ Engage in a regular morning routine.

_____ Engage in a relaxing evening routine.
_____ Keep up with routine medical care.
_____ Stretch or take short walks throughout the day.

Emotional/Psychological Self-Care

_____ Spend time with supportive people outside of work (and outside the field of law).
_____ Acknowledge your emotions (happy, sad, angry) rather than ignore them.
_____ Ask for help.
_____ Read literature that is unrelated to the law.
_____ Do something creative or learn something new.
_____ Say no to extra responsibilities if you do not have the time.
_____ Decrease stress where you can.
_____ Speak with a therapist.

Spiritual Self-Care

_____ Sing or listen to music.
_____ Meditate.
_____ Do yoga.
_____ Pray.
_____ Volunteer.

Professional Self-Care

_____ Take on assignments and other projects that are interesting and meaningful.
_____ Find a mentor.
_____ Leave the office for a period of time each day.
_____ Talk with former classmates/colleagues about work experiences.
_____ Set limits when possible.
_____ Take a "mental health" day or half day (or hour).
_____ Turn off your handheld device at bedtime.
_____ Set a consistent (yet flexible) work schedule.
_____ Create an office space that is comfortable for you.

I'm guessing that you are young and healthy. Let's keep it that way. Whether you adopt these suggestions or devise a system of your own, your health and wellness cannot be compromised. After all, in the end and despite everything we've learned here, the only thing that truly matters is your health.

19

ON LEADERSHIP

At the end of his book *Tribes: We Need You to Lead Us*, Seth Godin asks his readers for a favor. "If you got anything out of this book," he writes, "[g]ive this copy to someone else. Ask them to read it. Beg them to make a choice about leadership. We need them. We need you."[1]

My apologies to Mr. Godin. I could never part with my copy of *Tribes*. But I did hear him. Clearly. And I did make a choice about leadership. I wrote this book. I wrote it for you so that you could fully realize your potential and become a leader in your own right.

---

[1] Seth Godin, Tribes: We Need You to Lead Us (2008), at 147.

Many people in my position (seven years in a law firm) could write a book about the new lawyer experience. Most people in my position have the expertise, anyway. But I am the one who chose to write it. I am the one who chose to lead. And this is the final piece of advice I would like to share with you: Anyone can be a superstar associate. In fewer than 200 pages, you now know how. But not everyone will choose to be. And this is where your opportunity lies. By choosing to be the best lawyer you can be every day, by taking an affirmative and proactive approach to your career, by going above and beyond, by taking action to make sure that you matter from day one, you will be a top associate in your law firm and a leader in your practice area down the line, without question. If you do, if you make that choice to lead, I can say with confidence that our paths will cross. And I look forward to it.

APPENDIX 1
SAMPLE E-MAIL

To: Jenkins, Tom [client]

cc: Brady, John [law firm partner overseeing your work]

bcc:

From: You [associate]
Date: March 3, 2012

Re: *Atlantis Shops, Inc. v. Retail Express, Ltd.*—Breach of Contract Action—Renewed Discovery Deadline (3.21.2012)—Privileged and Confidential—Attorney-Client Communication—Do Not Forward

Mr. Jenkins [first correspondence with client],

My name is _____. I write to introduce myself as a new associate working on the *Atlantis Shops, Inc. v. Retail Express, Ltd.* litigation. I also write to update you on the status of discovery in the case and to make you aware of our renewed discovery deadline.

We are currently reviewing documents produced by Atlantis Shops and will have a detailed summary regarding the content of those documents to you by early next week.

Our new discovery deadline, as set by the court at a brief status hearing this morning, is March 21, 2012. Therefore, we will have until March 21 to supplement our original document production. Given the volume of documents, counsel for Atlantis Shops, Joe McKinley, has agreed to accept our supplemental production electronically in lieu of hard-copy documents.

Attached* please find a copy of the order issued at today's hearing. I will be in touch early next week with a detailed overview of the documents. In the interim, please do not hesitate to contact John or me if you have any questions.

Best regards,
You
Your Name
Firm Name
Address
Business Telephone
General Office Telephone Number [if different]
Cell Phone Number
Facsimile Number
E-mail Address
Office URL

*Stop! Do not write another word. Attach the document. Open the attachment to make sure that it is correct. Close the attachment. Continue writing.

BEFORE YOU SEND THE E-MAIL:

- ☐ Verify all e-mail addresses.
- ☐ Verify the spelling of all recipients' names.
- ☐ Proofread obsessively: verify that there are no typographical errors, grammatical errors, abbreviations, unnecessary exclamation points, or emoticons.
- ☐ Verify that you have included all attachments and that the attachments are correct.
- ☐ Privilege! Do not copy anyone outside your office on correspondence with your client. Do not forward any e-mails between you and your client to anyone outside the office.

APPENDIX 2
SAMPLE LETTER

Your Law Firm Letterhead

Your Name
Your E-mail
Your Direct Phone Number
Your Firm General Phone Number
March 21, 2012

Joseph McKinley
McKinley Law Firm
10 N. Delano St. #1405
Bakersfield, CA 93306
VIA: United States Mail and Messenger Delivery
Re: *Atlantis Shops, Inc. v. Retail Express, Ltd.*, Case No. 09-3181—Response to First Request for Production of Documents—Supplemental Production

Dear Mr. McKinley:

Per our agreement and as a supplement to Retail Express, Ltd.'s Response to Atlantis Shops, Inc.'s* First Request for Production of Documents, enclosed please find an electronic disk containing documents that are bates labeled RE027221-043210.

Please do not hesitate to contact me if you have any questions.

Yours truly,

_____ [signature]

You
cc: John Brady, Esq.

- - - [PAGE BREAK: ONE PAGE PER BCC RECIPIENT] - - -

bcc: Tom Jenkins, Esq.

*Note: If you use a party name more than once in letter correspondence, identify the party in shortened form after the first use of its name: Retail Express, Ltd. ("Retail Express").

BEFORE YOU SEND THE LETTER:

- ☐ Verify your own information.
- ☐ Verify recipient's information.
- ☐ Verify the spelling of recipient's name.
- ☐ Verify that the date of the letter is correct.
- ☐ Proofread in hard copy. Print the letter and read it carefully. Verify that there are no typographical errors, grammatical errors, abbreviations, and unnecessary exclamation points.
- ☐ Verify that you have included all enclosures and that the enclosures are correct.
- ☐ Verify the means for delivery of the letter.
- ☐ Privilege! Do not send a letter between you and your client to anyone outside the office.

APPENDIX 3
SAMPLE TIME ENTRIES

CLIENT	MATTER	DETAIL	DATE	TIME
This entry identifies the client. There is typically a corresponding number that is firm generated.	This entry identifies the matter that you are working on for a particular client. Any given client may have a corporate, tax, and litigation matter pending simultaneously.	This entry contains precise information about the work performed for the client. All entries must be meaningful. Do not include menial or administrative tasks in your billing entries. Bill accurately.	This entry identifies the date of the time entry.	This entry reflects the amount of time spent on a given task (or tasks) for a client.

Example 1

CLIENT	MATTER	DETAIL	DATE	TIME
Retail Express, Ltd. (1351777)	Breach of Contract Litigation (3117)	Researched California breach of contract laws and related statutory limitations; commenced drafting internal office memorandum to J. Brady regarding same.	March 1, 2012	2.7

The word *commenced* indicates that you are beginning a task. This shows that you are moving toward something. Subsequent entries should continue with this theme.

J. Brady: Choose a formal way to refer to all people mentioned in your time entries. Be consistent throughout. Follow any client-specific guidelines and preferences.

Example 2 (time entry for the following day)

CLIENT	MATTER	DETAIL	DATE	TIME
Retail Express, Ltd. (1351777)	Breach of Contract Litigation (3117)	Performed additional research regarding California breach of contract laws and related statutory limitations to clarify an apparent conflict in case law; continued drafting internal office memorandum to J. Brady regarding same.	March 2, 2012	3.5

Performed additional research and *continued drafting* show progression and reflect that you are working with purpose and moving forward toward accomplishing a goal and completing a task. State expressly why additional research was necessary. Subsequent entries should continue with this theme and end with *finalized internal office memorandum to J. Brady regarding same*.

Example 3 (includes communication with client)

CLIENT	MATTER	DETAIL	DATE	TIME
Retail Express, Ltd. (1351777)	Breach of Contract Litigation (3117)	Performed additional research regarding California breach of contract laws and related statutory limitations to clarify an apparent conflict in the law; continued drafting internal office memorandum to J. Brady regarding same; e-mail correspondence with T. Jenkins regarding discovery status and renewed discovery deadline of Mar. 21, 2012; follow-up telephone conference with T. Jenkins advising not to move forward with temporary restraining order in light of Atlantis's Feb. 3, 2012, letter indicating that it will refrain from selling merchandise until litigation is resolved.	March 3, 2012	3.5

State the specific method of communication with client: *e-mail correspondence with T. Jenkins* and *telephone conference with T. Jenkins*. Use the client's name rather than simply using *client*. State what was said/discussed and what was resolved, if possible. Although the general rule is to bill accurately and not arbitrarily round up or down in your billing, err on the side of billing less rather than more when you are billing for time spent with a client.

Example 4 (client requires task billing)

CLIENT	MATTER	DETAIL	DATE	TIME
Retail Express, Ltd. (1351777)	Breach of Contract Litigation (3117)	Performed additional research regarding California breach of contract laws and related statutory limitations to clarify an apparent conflict in the law (.5); continued drafting internal office memorandum to J. Brady regarding same (2.5); e-mail correspondence with T. Jenkins regarding discovery status and renewed discovery deadline of Mar. 21, 2012 (.2); follow-up telephone conference with T. Jenkins advising not to move forward with temporary restraining order in light of Atlantis's Feb. 3, 2012, letter indicating that it will refrain from selling merchandise until litigation is resolved (.3).	March 3, 2012	3.5

Task billing requires you to break down the amount of time spent on each task. If asked to bill this way, be sure that the tasks add up to your total time spent.

INDEX

A

Administrative assistants, 52–58, 67, 100
Alcohol consumption, 22
Alumni networking events, 108
Ancillary positions. *See* Associates and ancillary positions
Apologizing for mistakes, 101–2
Assignments, 61–72
    completing of, 66–67
    deadlines for, 44, 64–65, 71
    enthusiasm for, 23, 24, 70
    overall approach to, 71–72

       presenting of, 68–69
       soliciting of, 62–63
       taking credit for, 72
       taking of, 63–66
       turning down of, 69–71
Associates and ancillary positions, 32–34, 44
Attachments to e-mails, 83–84
Attire, 20–22
Attitude. *See* Mind-sets and attitudes

B

Bar associations, 108
Billing time, 89–92
       contingent fees, 90–91
       flat fee billing, 90
       hourly billing, 89–90
       importance of, 91–92
       methods of, 89–91
       mistakes and, 102
       partners and, 37
       profitability and, 15–16
       task billing, 134–35
Blackberries, 84
Bonuses, performance-based, 33, 35
Business cards, 107
Business casual, 20
Buying into the firm, 36

C

Calendaring of work assignments, 45–46, 65

Checklists

    calendar as, 45

    e-mail, 125

    letter writing, 129

    self-care inventory, 118–20

CLE (continuing legal education programs), 109–10

Clients

    attire and, 20–21

    billing time and, 92

    credits for, 38

    e-mail to, 83

    partners and, 35–36, 37

    servicing, 17

    speaking with, 75

Clothing, 20–22

Coaching, 1–2. *See also* Mentors

Commitments in careers, 7–9

Commuting to work, 21

Complaining about job, 110

Conflicts of interest, 112

Contacts, external, 107–8

Contingent fees, 90–91

Continuing legal education (CLE) programs, 109–10

Contract attorneys, 34

Contract partners, 36

Credits for client matters, 38

Criticism, 24
Cross-marketing, 108–9

D

Deadlines for assignments, 44, 64–65, 71
Delays, planning for, 44
Delegation of tasks, 47, 54
Demeanor, 22–23, 96
Depositions, 10–11
Drafts, turning in of, 69
Dress codes, 20–21

E

E-mails
    assignments and, 62, 67, 68–69
    checklist for, 125
    foreign languages and, 76
    miscellaneous advice on, 85–86
    organizing, 50
    responding to, 85
    sample e-mail, 123–25
    turning off, 47
    writing of, 80–84
Emotional self-care, 119
Enthusiasm for work assignments, 23, 24, 70
Equity buy-ins, 36
Equity partners, 36–37
Esq., use of, 88

Ethics rules, 112, 113

F

Facebook, 114. *See also* Social media
Federal Rules, 89
Feedback, 93–97
    absence of, 94
    abundance of, 94–95
    completing assignments and, 67
    yearly reviews and, 95–97
Files, organization of, 49–50
Flat fee billing, 90
Flip-flops, 22
Foreign languages, 76–77
Formal settings, speaking in, 74

G

Generational differences, 25–26
Goal setting, 10–11, 96–97
Godin, Seth, 4, 121
Good impressions, 62, 64
Google, 114

H

Handheld devises, 84
Headphones, 23
Health and wellness, 117–20
    emotional/psychological, 119

　　　　physical, 118–19
　　　　professional, 119–20
　　　　self-care inventory and, 118–20
　　　　spiritual, 119
Hourly billing, 89–90

I

Impression, making a good. *See* Good impressions
Income partners, 35–36
Informal settings, speaking in, 73–74
In-house positions, 29
Interpersonal skills, 23–26, 28–29
Introducing yourself, 62–63
iPhones, 84

J

Junior associates, 32–33, 44

L

Lateral partners, 36
Law firm roles, 13–17
　　　　profit generation and, 15–17
　　　　servicing clients, 17
　　　　as support staff for senior attorneys, 14, 16–17
Law firm structures, 31–38
　　　　associates and ancillary positions, 32–34
　　　　attorney designations and, 32–37
　　　　firm size and, 32

      partner positions, 34–37
      promotions and, 30, 38
Law journals, publishing articles in, 109
Leadership, 121–22
Legal news, keeping up with, 106–7, 115
Legal pads, 49
Legal secretaries. *See* Administrative assistants
Legal writing. *See* Writing like a lawyer
Letter writing, 86–89
      sample, 127–29
Limited liability partnerships, 32
LinkedIn, 114. *See also* Social media
Lists, keeping organized with, 50
Litigation vs. transactional practice, 27–30

M

Mail services, 89
Maintaining perspective, 11
Marketing, 103–10
      external, 107–9
      internal, 104–7
Mentors, 39–41
      administrative assistants and, 58
      completing assignments and, 67, 71
      feedback and, 94
      goal setting and, 10
      mistakes, on how to handle, 101
      self-care and, 120

speaking with opposing counsel and, 76
Midlevel associates, 33
Mind-sets and attitudes, 7–11
    commitments and, 7–9
    goal setting and, 9–11
    maintaining perspective and, 11
    taking assignments and, 63
Mistakes, 96, 99–102
Moore, Desirée, 137

N

Networking events, 108
New lawyer experience, 3–5
The New Yorker on coaching, 1
Nonbillable work, 105
Note taking, 80

O

Of counsel attorneys, 33–34
Office organization, 48
One-tiered partnership systems, 34–35
Open-door policies, 23
Opposing counsel, speaking with, 75–76
Organization, 47–50. *See also* Time management
    importance of, 47–48
    in office, 48
    substantive practice and, 49–50
    tips for, 48–49

Out-of-office replies, 86

P

Panicking, 100–101
Paperless offices, 48
Paralegals, 58–59
Partner positions and systems, 34–37. *See also* Promotion tracks
Phones. *See* Telephones
Photocopies, distribution of, 75
Physical self-care, 118–19
Policies of law firms, 105–6
Practice groups, mentors from, 40–41
Professionalism, 19–26
        attire and, 20–22
        demeanor and, 22–23
        interpersonal skills and, 23–26
Professional self-care, 119–20
Profitability, 15–17
Promotion tracks, 30, 38. *See also* Partner positions and systems
Proofreading, 84, 125, 129
Psychological self-care, 119
Publishing articles, 109

R

Reliability, 24–25
Reviews
        of administrative assistants, 55–56
        annual, 95–97

S

Salaries, 15–16, 30, 32–33

Salutations in writing, 82, 87

Secretaries. *See* Administrative assistants

Self-care, 118–20

Senior associates, 33, 34–35

Senior attorneys
- administrative assistants and, 53
- as clients, 17
- of counsel and, 34
- deference for, 25–26
- reviews and, 96
- support staff for, 14, 16–17

Shoes, 21–22

Size of firms, 32

Social media, 111–16
- legal news on, 106, 115
- legal practice enhancement and, 113–17
- professional use of, 112–13
- time management and, 47

Solo practitioner, role as, 17, 62

Speaking like a lawyer, 73–77
- clients and, 75
- colleagues in formal settings and, 74
- colleagues in informal settings and, 73–74
- foreign languages and, 76–77
- opposing counsel and, 75–76

Spiritual self-care, 119

Staff, working with, 51–59. *See also* Support staff, new lawyer's role as

    administrative assistants and, 52–58
        basics of relationship with, 52–55
        change of, 56–58
        reviews of, 55–56
    other staff and, 59
    paralegals and, 58–59

Structure of law firms. *See* Law firm structures
Suits as law firm attire, 20–21
Support staff, new lawyer's role as, 14, 16–17. *See also* Staff, working with

T

Task billing, 134–35
Teamwork, 63
Telephones
    messages, 80
    returning calls, 87
Time management, 43–47. *See also* Organization
    importance of, 44–46
    sample time entries, 131–35
    tips for, 46–47
Time sheets, 91
Transactional practice vs. litigation, 27–30
Tribes, lawyers as, 4–5
Tribes: We Need You to Lead Us (Godin), 121
Trust, mentors and, 41

Twitter, 115–16. *See also* Social media
Two-tiered partnership systems, 35

U

Utilization rates, 15–16

V

Vacations, scheduling of, 71
Verbal communication skills. *See* Speaking like a lawyer

W

Wellness. *See* Health and wellness
Work assignments. *See* Assignments
Work ethic, 25
Work-life balance, 118
Writing like a lawyer, 79–89
        e-mails, 80–86. *See also* E-mails
        letter writing and, 86–89, 127–29
        litigation and, 28
        note taking and, 80

Y

YouTube, 114–15. *See also* Social media

ABOUT THE AUTHOR

Desirée Moore is an author, speaker, and attorney. She is the President and founder of Greenhorn Legal, LLC (www.greenhornlegal.com), which provides practical skills training for law students and new lawyers nationwide as they transition from academics into their legal careers. Ms. Moore is also the founder of Greenhorn Bold, a presentation, presence, and communication skills training program for lawyers and non-lawyers alike (www.greenhornbold.com), and an Adjunct Professor at Loyola University Chicago School of Law. She can be reached via email at desiree@greenhornlegal.com or via Twitter at @greenhornlegal.